Teaching the Students of the 2020s

Classroom Wisdom From a Master Teacher

Bruce Hansen

Illustrations by Kelly Hansen

Mt. Hood Press, Portland, Oregon USA

Comments by Top Professionals in Teaching, Mentoring, Teacher Education and Administration

"This book gives practical (and easy-to-implement) ways to reframe and change pedagogical and behavioral approaches in order to yield positive student outcomes. A must-read for new teachers!"

Sarah K. McMahan, Ph.D.
Professor and Director, Office of Clinical Practice Texas Women's University,
College of Professional Education

"Through direct writing, succinct summaries, and easily understood anecdotes, Hansen both reminds veteran teachers and encourages new teachers to incorporate tried-and-true practices in the classroom. His writing reads not like a textbook, but truly like wisdom to be passed on by a master teacher."

Todd Knight
2022 Idaho Teacher of the Year

"Teaching the Students of the 2020s is filled with reminder nuggets on how to be an effective teacher in the classroom in today's tumultuous climate. I found it easy to read, relevant, and resourceful . . . a quick guide for navigating the many situations that come up in our classrooms on a daily basis. This book could easily be a must-read for any teacher, new or seasoned, every year before school begins."

Sharita Ware
2022 Indiana Teacher of the Year
MS Engineering and Technology Education

"At a time when there is high turnover in the teaching profession and when teachers are faced with the many impacts of Covid, this book offers a critical helping hand to educators. Every chapter provides easy to understand solutions for everyday classroom behaviors and challenges. Teachers need positive, real life examples of how to support and engage their students and they can find those throughout Teaching the Students of the 2020's."

Susan Castillo
Former Oregon Superintendent
of Public Instruction

"Bruce Hansen shares authentic classroom realities, but more importantly he shares strategies for actionable solutions for the novice and the veteran teacher."

Karen Corcoran, Associate Professor of Instruction
Regional Coordinator of
Professional Internships in Teaching
Middle Childhood Education Program
Coordinator / The Gladys W. & David H. Patton
College of Education / Ohio University

In his book, Bruce Hansen outlines numerous strategies and approaches to enable teachers to create a safe, engaging and exciting environment for students. His many anecdotes, illustrations and quotes provide authentic examples of the situations that teachers encounter daily and how they can be approached with professionalism and compassion. The 3 R's of classroom interactions are highlighted and elaborated upon: routines, relationships and rules (expectations). The book is well-organized and enables the reader to access the valuable information that is provided. This wisdom that comes from his many years in the classroom is truly evident in the topics, writing style, and advice offered on this readable book.

Ellen Baker M.Ed
Director of Educator Licensure Programs
Chair of VCEPP
Licensure Officer College of
Education & Social Services
University of Vermont
Education Department

"The post-pandemic classroom requires additional attention to classroom management practices. Bruce Hansen delivers a timely work that guides beginner teachers in addressing the challenges associated with the always-developing social, emotional, and academic needs of diverse classroom communities. This work provides its readers with guided steps and solutions to classroom challenges. A must-have for any novice teacher and the emerging skills essential to empowering the learning of students through guidance and teacher-agency."

Dr. Jessica Slade
Regents 2020 Outstanding Teaching Award Recipient /
Assistant Professor of Instruction Department of Teacher
Education
The University of Texas at El Paso

"Teaching the Students of the 2020s contains practical and pertinent advice on a wide range of issues facing educators today. Whether you are brand new to the profession or a veteran teacher, this book provides proven and tested ideas and guidance for teaching in our current culture and climate. It is organized in such a way that makes it fast and easy to locate suggestions and solutions for a given situation or problem. Keep this book handy as an excellent "how-to" resource for beginning and finishing a year well, and everything in between."

Bret Dockter
2022 North Dakota Teacher of the Year
6th Grade Teacher
HWC Head Football Coach

"Bruce Hansen's 36-year career in classrooms has informed his latest text that offers a common-sense approach to classroom management that is grounded by connections with learners. This ready reference provides practical techniques and authentic case studies that will resonate with both seasoned and novice educators. Read it from start to finish, but also keep this book at hand for on-demand solutions for everyday classroom challenges."

Tammy Pawloski, Ph.D.
Francis Marion University
Professor of Education
Director, Center of Excellence to Prepare
Teachers of Children of Poverty

"In my work in teacher education and teacher professional development, I am always asked to make theory and research in teacher education accessible to practitioners. The connection between theory and practice is paramount to the translation of quality professional development to the classroom for real change. This book makes educational theory and research accessible to all teachers. It is a very practical and authentic experience of what teaching involves and stays grounded in the voices of real students and teachers. This book makes teaching accessible to new teachers and veteran teachers looking for new ideas to change their teaching practices. What is clear in reading the book is that it is written by a true practitioner who spent 30+ years learning from first hand accounts about what it means to be a teacher."

Dr. Eugenia Mora-Flores
Assistant Dean of Teacher Education
Professor of Clinical Education
University of Southern California
Rossier School of Education

"When wisdom meets years of experience in the classroom, the result is Teaching Students of the 2020s. Teaching Students of the 2020s is a 36 year journey into the world of education. Hansen's experience throughout elementary and middle school takes the form of advice for new and veteran teachers, explicit examples of classroom management, real classroom scenarios and possible strategies to approach both academic and behavioral situations. These resources are organized in sections that guide the reader through a variety of aspects that embody the world of teaching, from strategies, activities, differentiation, safety, family engagement and lesson planning. Hansen's comprehensive approach to teaching takes the form of this book that will support educators in any stage of their teaching journey."

Marta García
Massachusetts Teacher of the Year 2022

Mt. Hood Press
www.mthoodpress.com
info@mthoodpress.com

The recommendations and suggestions in this book are the author's and were synthesized and formed as a result of decades of experience and exposure to a vast and deep exploration of other teacher's techniques, authors, books, articles and studies that have coalesced into the author's opinions. Any attempt to disaggregate the origins of any one strategy or recommendation would likely result in such a high degree of guesswork, that the citation would be inaccurate. My apologies to the unaccredited sources who did the hard work of coming before me, and my deep thanks for helping me find my way. Readers are encouraged to browse the *Books for Support* page to find paths to build their own classroom management skills.

All the models and case studies are based on real teachers and students, but the names have been changed.

Other Writings by the Author

Journal/Magazine Articles:

Educational Leadership

Reading Today

Journal of Social & Emotional Learning

Illinois School Journal

Education Week

also scores of travel articles in mainstream motorcycle and kayak magazines.

Books:

Literature Based Writing Instruction

Motorcycle Journeys Through the Pacific Northwest

Ride Guide to America (contributor)

Novels under the pen name, Tyler Blackthorne

Denali

Arctic Forces

Arctic Protocol

About the Author

I've been a public school teacher for 36 years and taught every grade level from first to eighth. Some of those schools were in inner-city high-poverty neighborhoods, some in suburban wealthy areas and many in mixed neighborhoods. For 30 years I've taught graduate level classes for educators, ten of these years as a college supervisor of candidates learning teaching skills. I've been in hundreds of classrooms and taught hundreds of educators. I've presented at conferences all over the country, taught classes or seminars for Portland State University, University of Oregon and Pacific University, and provided staff development for various districts. What really makes me a Master Teacher, is that I'm still learning.

Some of the awards I've received include: An Award of Excellence from the National Teachers Hall of Fame, a commendation from the Governor of Oregon, a Sustained Superior Performance Award and two Golden Apple Awards from my school districts for excellence in teaching. I was an advisor to Oregon's Superintendent of Public Instruction, Susan Castillo as a member of her "Brain Trust".

Probably the most precious award I've ever gotten was from 9 year-old James who started the school year by telling me he hated school, and it was jail. At year's end, he gave me a *Get Out of Jail Free* card and a hug telling me he loved me and my class.

In my spare time, my wife and I love to travel, visit family, and take pictures.

Preface

The 2020s Students and Educators

Students attempting to deal with disruptions to their routines, education, and family life often show their reactions in ways ranging from stubborn indifference to classroom violence. These stress reactions are particularly destructive to academic progress in low-income communities which are already under duress from poverty. When low-resourced students face the stress from millions in Covid deaths, loss of family, Zoom schooling, a pandemic, learning alone at home or with stressed family, anti-vaccination misinformation, school shootings, computer/internet problems and so forth, it is expected they will have learning problems.

Educators are stressed from the Covid pandemic, screamers at school board meetings, dropping enrollment, attacks on public education, lower test scores, rising absenteeism, lack of subs and paraprofessionals, political types blaming teachers for perceived school failures, and concerns about their family's health and safety. Right now, it seems to be good politics to blame teachers for problems over which they have no control. A recent study showed 90% of teachers contemplating leaving the profession. The profession is in crisis.

It is my hope that this book will boost teaching skills to make teaching less stressful and more fun. I offer strategies and techniques to settle and teach the K-12 children of the 2020s and urge you to care for yourself.

The focus of this book is on in-person instruction of a general education population mostly directed at grades 3 - 8, but there's something for everyone. Some children are so affected by stress, that they will need extra help in addition to what works with general education students. Teachers can not be expected to work miracles, but they often do.

Emotionally healthy students will also find it easier to learn and retain knowledge when in a classroom where the teacher uses or adapts the suggestions in this book.

Foreward

The familiar warning for new teachers, "Don't smile until December" is, of course, not advisable for any teacher, veteran or new, and is not intended to be taken literally. In Teaching the Students of the 2020s, Bruce Hansen offers tremendously practical advice for simultaneously sustaining students' attention, ensuring their optimal learning, making learning a joyful experience for all, and yes, even smiling before Christmas and throughout the year.

One of the first post-pandemic books addressing classroom management, this book is witty, engaging, profound, and beautifully written by a master teacher who has talked the talk and walked the walk. The author has taught grades one through eight and has devoted the last decade to teaching at the college level and supervising pre-service educators. The recipient of several teaching awards at the school district, state, and national levels, Bruce Hansen has proven again and again that he understands classroom management and, more importantly, possesses astute knowledge about learners and how to motivate and engage them. As Hansen recollects, a third-grade student in his class once equated school with "Jail." However, this student was so inspired by Mr. Hansen that he handed Mr. Hansen a "Get out of Jail Free" card at the end of the school year and told Mr. Hansen that he loved him and now loved school. Likewise, this book will equally inspire readers who find teaching unbelievably challenging to "get out of jail, free" as well.

This well organized 11-chapter book is complete with text boxes that emphasize important points in the chapter readings. It also includes many examples of teachers and students engaging in taxing situations that every new and veteran teacher will encounter and wonder exactly how to handle. For example, the book provides a candid account of the author's first year of teaching and how his principal planned to fire him because of his obvious lack of classroom management skills. Motivated by his principal's words and pending "early retirement," Bruce Hansen explains the strategies that he enlisted that not only allowed him to continue to teach, but also enabled him to become a master teacher.

Teachers today are facing many challenges. They are underpaid and under appreciated. Many teachers, especially those working in urban schools, endure overly large class sizes, insufficient resources, including teaching assistants, books, technology, and supplies, unruly student behavior, uninvolved families, and deplorable environmental conditions. It is no wonder, then, that over 40% of teachers leave the teaching profession within their first five years of teaching and, for teachers working in low socio-economic schools, the resignation rate is 50% within the first five years of teaching. "Teachers are toiling in the dark without praise or recognition," laments Hansen. The teaching market is desperate to hire qualified new teachers to fill the void left by early resignations and to meet the needs of the un*derserved and yet very deserving students.*

*Teaching the Stude*nts of the 2020's offers a bright ray of hope for this presently dire situation in the teaching profession. As a veteran teacher of preschool and elementary grades for eight years and a university professor and student teaching supervisor for 38 years, I immediately recognized this book you are holding as an invaluable resource. I found myself nodding my head and saying, "uh-huh" as I turned the book's pages and book-marked every other page. My upcoming student teaching group at the University of Rhode Island will relish the techniques that Bruce Hansen advocates and the young students and I, as their professor, will also reap the bountiful rewards bestowed upon us by this gem of a book. As teachers, nationwide, recognize their power to "turn around a lost child," ignite a passion for learning," and "set a child on the right path for a successful life" (Hansen, 2022), we can all thank this book's author, Bruce Hansen for igniting in us this same passion for teaching.

> **Foreward By**
>
> **Susan Trostle Brand**
>
> Susan Trostle Brand is a professor of Education at the University of Rhode Island and has been a PreK- 16 educator for over 50 years. Dr. Brand is the author/ editor of four textbooks and numerous book chapters, articles and presentations and serves as a United Nations representative for Kappa Delta Pi National Education Honor Society.

Contents

1

Teacher and Student Expectations

TOPICS ADDRESSED IN THIS CHAPTER:

- EXPECT SUCCESS

- SHOWING YOUR EXPECTATIONS

- SHOULD YOU HYPNOTIZE YOUR STUDENTS?

- REINFORCING CLASSROOM SUCCESS

- NEVER GIVE STUDENTS A NEGATIVE ROLE TO PLAY

- 5 WAYS TO USE POSITIVE EXPECTATIONS TO HELP STUDENTS BUILD A CONSTRUCTIVE SELF-IMAGE

- USING STUDENT SUGGESTIBILITY AND POSITIVE ROLES TO IMPROVE BEHAVIORAL AND ACADEMIC OUTCOMES

- CASE STUDY: SHELBY

> *You need to find the place where your students can succeed and where they also believe you have confidence in their abilities.*

Extra space for reader's notes:

If You Don't Expect Success, You Won't be Disappointed

Expectations are so important that I put this chapter at the beginning of the book. Most books start with an introductory chapter, and I wrote that, but I didn't want to start the book with it. I wanted to start with what you can do right now to help your students learn regardless of how stressed they are. The introductory chapter, if you are interested is actually Chapter 12.

As you read this, decide how you can help your students develop positive expectations for themselves.

Make a decision to use your expectations to improve your students' performance.

When you first meet your students, expect them to work hard and become successful learners. If

you expect your students to do poorly, you are actually putting an additional barrier in front of them. Besides all their other learning problems, they must also get past your low expectations. This chapter offers suggestions to help you show high expectations and convey those to your students.

Showing Your Expectations

An effective teacher exudes a belief that students will attempt to follow directions. When students fall short of this expectation, a competent teacher might show surprise, disappointment, incredulity or use other reactions that signal high expectations. The suggestions below work when you've established a trusting relationship with your students.

Surprise: "Why Jerome! Are you still just sitting there? I thought for sure you'd be working on your outline. Let's figure out what's holding you back."

Disappointment: "Oh Jerome. I so expected you to have more done on your outline. You are probably thinking this is like other classes. It's not. This is fifth grade. We do our outlines in this class. Let's figure out what's holding you back."

Incredulity: "Huh? Jerome! I can't believe this is all you have done. I know you are better than this. Let's figure out what's holding you back and get you where you want to be."

A Student's Role

You might notice that in the above examples, the teacher sometimes gives Jerome a positive role to play. Embracing a role can raise student expectations and help a

> *An effective teacher exudes a belief that students will attempt to follow directions.*

student persevere when things get hard. After telling a student what their role is, you should look for times when that student is fulfilling that role and point it out. When you hold your students accountable for their actions, you are showing them that you have high expectations for them.

Giving a student a role to play, like that of a successful second grader, is different from attempting to convince a student that broccoli is their favorite, when they hate it. You'll lose credibility. So when giving a student a personal role, like longing to complete work on time, be sure there's some truth to it.

High expectations also means you give students who've fallen behind, perhaps due to Covid, a reasonable chance to stay with the class. Break their goals into more approachable targets that you can reasonably expect them to reach. For example, when every student in your class can read silently for 20 minutes, and Beth shoots out of her chair after 4 minutes, you can give her a goal of 5 minutes for the next time, and help her track her progress.

Should you Hypnotize Your Students?

Flash back to my second year as a teacher. The assistant superintendent of our district came into my classroom after school and asked if I wanted to participate in some training where I would learn to hypnotize my students. Being only 23 years old and lacking good judgment, I agreed to go.

> *Jennifer looked down at the book, her eyes sparkling. She got it. I didn't hypnotize her, but I did made suggestions on how she should feel.*

After the training, I was informed that the program had ended and the assistant superintendent had been fired for starting up the scheme. And under no circumstances should I ever hypnotize a student. I never have.

However, in that training I learned that people in

a relaxed state are more responsive to suggestions. Children are already very susceptible to suggestions, so I propose you use your students' suggestibility to help them adopt a positive role for themselves.

So should you hypnotize your students?

No.

Parents don't want you to do this. Your school board doesn't want you to do this. Your principal will likely have to fire you if you do this. It could have profoundly negative consequences on your students.

Let's think about using the suggestibility of children to improve educational and social outcomes.

I was teaching in a school where students had a wide range of economic resources. I noticed that students had an ability that the others didn't: they could self-reinforce.

> " *Let's think about using the suggestibility of children to improve educational and social outcomes.*

For example, if a well-nurtured, emotionally healthy child completed a terrific project, he would deservedly demonstrate pride in his accomplishment. He likely learned this when his family modeled pride in an accomplishment.

I remember when I was trying to teach a non-reading fourth grader how to read, there came a day when Jennifer read a chapter book all by herself. I asked her how she felt, and just got a shrug. To me, this was a colossal achievement.

I suggested to her that she should feel proud and capable. She should feel like she's taking control over her learning, and feel a rush of power.

Jennifer looked down at the book, her eyes sparkling. She got it. I didn't hypnotize her, but I did make suggestions on how she should feel about having pride.

Using Student Suggestibility and Positive Roles to Improve Behavioral and Academic Outcomes

Expect your students to improve and do well. I know you can do this.

• *Communicate this to them by avoiding ability grouping. These groups can make members feel like you lack confidence in their chance at improvement.*

• *Express surprise or puzzlement when they don't make a reasonable effort. "Why Bobbie, this isn't like you to give up so easily. Fourth graders try harder. You are a fourth grader; therefore you must try just a tiny bit harder. Can you do that?"*

• *Help them see themselves as capable people "Bobbie, I know you can do this. I watched you write that wonderful essay last week. That's who you are: a capable person."*

• *Show surprise at misbehavior and explain to them they are better than that. Tell them who they truly are "Bobbie, I can't believe you broke her pencil. You've outgrown that behavior. Now as a fourth grader, you don't do things like that. You need to relax and fall back into your fourth grade behavior, not this silly third grade stuff like breaking people's pencils."*

• *Show them proof of their progress and tell them how this shows who they are and what they believe "Bobbie, look at this chart you made! This shows you are a good student who cares about his work. I want you to look at this chart and feel proud of yourself and realize you are a true fourth grader."*

• *Teach them how to self-reinforce so they feel good when making progress or accomplishing something "Bobbie, every time you complete an assignment, I want you to look at it and feel proud of yourself and realize how you are growing up to be a better student."*

• Give your students attainable goals and attempt to make sure they accomplish them. Use language that makes progress seem possible. "Bobbie, I know you can try just a little bit harder," is better than, "Bobbie, you need to accomplish this goal." The latter can seem overwhelming, but trying just a "little bit harder" can seem doable to your students.

Reinforcing Classroom Success

How do you know when you are riding a bike correctly? It just feels right. Students need to know how a pleasant, well-functioning classroom feels. Maybe one of your behavior signals is FREEZE!

> " *When you tell your students that they should decide to do well, they raise their own expectations for their behavior.*

I have "frozen" my class when they are behaving perfectly and told them that this is what they should expect in our class: hardworking students who are enjoying their learning and working together harmoniously. I tell them they should feel good about their behavior and decide that next time we have independent work, this is how they will approach the time.

When you tell your students that they should decide to do well, they raise their own expectations for their behavior.

Case Study: Shelby

Shelby entered my third grade class wearing her ever present *I Love Soccer* shirt. It soon became apparent

> " *Use language that makes progress seem possible.*

that her academic achievement lagged behind most of her classmates.

In order for her to be successful, nearly all her assignments needed to be modified.

The following year, I taught fourth and was happy to see sweet Shelby on my list. As we started our first social studies unit, I assigned a mapping project, and then monitored classroom progress carefully to see which students needed modifications. I considered starting Shelby with a modified project, but decided to watch to see if and where she stumbled.

From her perspective, it seemed that I expected her to perform like all her classmates. To my surprise, instead of needed modifications, Shelby did just fine. It was like she had emerged from a cocoon and become a butterfly. Nearly none of her assignments needed to be modified in fourth grade. Shelby had simply matured. Imagine her progress if I had automatically given her a simpler project based on my earlier expectations.

A teacher needs to know when to make adjustments to get the most out of each student. The art of teaching demands that a teacher knows when to make these changes. If I had known with certainty that Shelby would need modifications, it would have been counterproductive to let her needlessly struggle before modifying her assignments. However, with high expectations, I closely monitored each student so I could catch any of them before they failed. This gave Shelby the chance to show me what she could do.

> **Your students need a role.**

Part of having high expectations is acting confident in your students' successes when you can't actually convince yourself that your students will succeed. This is not to say you blow them away with something so ambitious that it will make them unable to succeed. You need to find the place where your students can succeed and where they also believe you have confidence in their abilities.

This is called finding the place where students can learn to struggle productively and not just give up when things get frustrating.

Part of having high expectations is acting confident in your students' successes when you can't actually convince yourself that your students will succeed.

If you keep pushing the message that you know your students can improve, it will help them internalize a feeling that progress is possible.

Never Give Students a Negative Role to Play

Your students need a role. They are young, and don't know who they are. Most students look to the adults in their lives to form their view of themselves. Here are some things you should never say to yourself or your students. Kids will adopt your negative expectations and not let you down if you expect them to fail.

If you keep pushing the message that you know your students can improve, it will help them internalize a feeling that progress is possible. Students with this view are more likely to rebound from failure or negative feedback.

5 Teacher Comments that Will Make Learning Hard for Your Students:

> *1.   This is the worst class I've ever taught.*
>
> *2.   I know it's really hard to concentrate during 8th period.*
>
> *3.   Since it's the day before the holiday, it's hard for you to learn.*
>
> *4.   Since it's the day after Halloween, the sugar high you are feeling will make it hard for you to behave.*
>
> *5.   To class or student: You are so _____. Fill in the blank with: stubborn, lazy, negative, destructive, or other negative role for them to fill.*
>
> *You may think that Sam is lazy, but don't tell him about your thoughts in a way that gives him a role to play. Using the above principles of high expectations, you can say things like, "Sam, when you act like this, some people might think you are not trying hard, but I know you do try. I've seen you on the playground."*

5 Ways to Use Positive Expectations to Help Students Build a Constructive Self-Image

You don't want to overtly lie to your class. They will see right through this, but you can influence their perceptions—especially if you cite evidence that your statement is true. These are most effective if you use them after the class sees clear evidence to support your comments.

What you should say to your class or student(s)

to help them develop a positive self-image:

1. I've noticed that this class really loves to learn. But hey, that's who you are, kids who love to learn.

2. It really makes you feel good when you get so much done. You love to be productive. It makes you feel proud.

3. You called her a name? That's not like you. You like to make your classmates feel good. Like yesterday when you told Jane you liked her drawing. When you call people names, it will make you feel bad about yourself. Don't do it.

4. When you see your artwork up on the board, you are going to feel proud of yourself. After a while, that pride will help you persevere when a different assignment gets more difficult.

5. This is seventh grade math; we don't make rude sounds here. You are here to learn, not cause trouble. When you cause trouble, you aren't acting like a seventh grader. If you're making rude sounds, you are probably thinking this is like sixth grade math. If you think that, you are wrong. Seventh graders act respectfully to their teachers and classmates.

2

The Safe Classroom

It's hard to underestimate the value to the 2020s' learner of making sure your class is a safe place. When students enter your class, they know that they need not fear humiliation or other physical or emotional harm. They know you will protect them from any such dangers.

As you read, think about how you could adapt any of these suggestions to make your class a safer and better place to learn.

A safe teacher is predictable, consistent and fair. This teacher avoids using sarcasm, humiliation or other destructive student control techniques and avoids yelling or showing any loss of control, except when strategic. Thus, it's OK to cry at the end of an emotional novel, but not to loose control when a student tells you he's being abused. The latter is when your student needs to you to be empathetic, but strong. Students may be more in need of a safe, predictable teacher when adjusting to stress caused by a health crisis, poverty or other disruptive forces.

Creating a Safe Classroom

You make it clear that in your class, it's OK to make a mistake. Students should not fear that their learning and/or behavioral problems are discussed with other students on the playground or lunch break. Of course, they are free to discuss anything that disturbs them with their families and the school staff.

A safe classroom does not mean that students do not face consequences for their inappropriate choices. They need to count on it. For most children, being safe also means that they know their teacher will be respectful and consistent. The boundaries will not change no matter how much a student tests them. A teacher who runs a class with squishy/inconsistent boundaries often has anxious, boundary-testing students instead of settled students.

Once you've established your classroom as safe, your students will begin to take academic risks — the most productive learning behavior. They will feel confident about venturing out to the limits of their knowledge and abilities. Timid and emotionally fragile students gain the most from a safe classroom.

> *A safe classroom does not mean that students do not face consequences for their inappropriate choices. They need to count on it.*

Starting a Safe Classroom

One of my go-to first day of school activities is a game I play with my students where I identify a playing card that's randomly drawn out of a deck. I use this game to show that it's OK to make a mistake in my class, and to reinforce my class rules about when to raise a hand to contribute and when to just call out an answer.

Card Trick to start a safe class: Naming a randomly drawn card from a deck

Announce that you will be able to name a card drawn from a deck. Here's how to start:

1. Make a T-Chart with Right Answer on one side and Wrong Answer on the other.

2. Make a show of shuffling a deck of cards and have a respected student draw a card, but not show it to you. Turn your back and have the student show the class the card. Have your students record the card then cover the up so you can't see it.

3. Ask: "*Do I know what this card is?*" You want the class to be clear that you have no idea of which card was drawn.

4. Make statements to eliminate half of the cards with each of your guesses. Here's how the statements might go if the card was the 3 of spades. Start by saying:

A.   "*The card is red.*" Students will say that's wrong. In the Wrong side of the T-Chart, write "red".

B. Model your thinking by talking aloud, "*I know the card isn't red, so it must be a club or a spade because they are black. The card is a spade.*" Students will confirm this, so write, "spade" on the T-Chart under the Right column.

Right Answer	Wrong Answer
spade	red
3	8, 9, 10, J, Q, K
	4, 5, 6, 7
	ace or 2

C.   *"OK, I know the card is a spade, so I'll see if I can narrow it down. The card is an 8, 9, 10, J, Q, or K."* The class will tell you this is wrong, so you record it on the T-Chart.

D.   *"Now I know the card must be lower than an 8, so I'll guess. The card is a 4, 5, 6, or 7 of spades."* Wrong. Record this in the Wrong column.

E.   *"Now I know the card must be an Ace, 2, 3 or 4 of spades. The card is an Ace or 2."* Wrong. Record this in the Wrong column.

F.   Make a show of studying the T-Chart. *"Hmm. So now I know that the card must be a 3 or 4 of spades. It's a 3."* Students will be excited. Right! Triumphantly you turn over the drawn card and show the class a 3 of spades.

"I got a lot of wrong answers, but I'm proud of what I've learned through the wrong answers. This is our fifth grade class. It's a safe class. You can get a wrong answer in here, because in this class, there's no shame in making a mistake. You can learn as much from a wrong answer as a right one. Throughout this year, you will make some mistakes and get some answers wrong, but you won't let that bother you, because you are now fifth grader, and that's how fifth graders learn."

> *You can get a wrong answer here, because in this class, there's no shame in making a mistake.*

Simple Classroom Rules/Guidelines

It's possible to lay out a complex web of rules that might tangle you up and make it easy for students to manipulate them. I suggest you have simple rules that are broad enough to apply to any situation. If you have a rule that says you can't throw pencils in class, and someone throws a pen, then claims it wasn't specifically against the rules, you could be in for an argument.

Some teachers like to spend a class period, or longer, making up classroom rules. Personally, I would rather use the time to teach something. It's my class and these are my rules: **Be Safe, Be Kind, Be Respectful.** .

When TJ throws a pencil across the room, you can point to Be Safe, and explain that he's getting a consequence because he broke the first rule in your class. Truly any kind of destructive behavior a student might come up with, is covered by these rules.

I would suggest spending some time discussing the reasoning behind each rule and get student input about how they'd like the rules to work in your classroom

Responding to a Wrong Answer

You show your students the problem 2+2 and say, "*Raise your hand when you think you know the answer.*"
You pause until nearly all students have their hand up, and then call on Alexis.

She confidently calls out, "*Five!*"

> **Classroom Rules**
> Be Safe
> Be Kind
> Be Respectful

What should your response be? You want to preserve her confidence and willingness to participate, and you want other students to see that it's safe to give a wrong answer in your class.

When a student gives a wrong answer, you can protect their self-esteem by asking her to explain how she got to that answer. If you do this, she's likely to figure out where her thinking is flawed and you can praise her.

"Alexis, you are thinking of 2+3. This is 2+2. Help me understand how to got 5."

Students need to know if they are falling short of your learning goals. If Alexis can't find her error, the best way to discuss this is to tell her what parts she got right, and what she can do to learn the rest. Express confidence that your students can learn the material.

Your goal in responding to a wrong answer is to maintain the feeling of safety in your class, and to clearly get the correct answer out to your students.

Grouping for Instruction - The Low Group

This is the group, made up of **general education students**, that none of your students want to be in. Don't fool yourself into thinking no one knows which group is low — they know. Some students, and their families, may view inclusion in the low group as a mark of shame or humiliation. Being in this group is a disincentive to attend school, and hits a student hard that their teacher thinks they are less capable.

A recent powerful study of the effects on students placed in "low" groups came up with this conclusion: "We argue that this is a symbolically violent process that negatively impacts the psychosocial positioning of children as they negotiate their identities within the figured world of the primary school classroom. This in turn influences their learner identities, as well as their perceptions of their ability to learn." (McGillicuddy, Devine, Dympna, 2020)

You don't lie to your low students and tell them they are just fine. But you don't make it public. Evidence suggests that, despite the best intentions, we teachers will expect lower achievement from members of a low group.

> *Having a static low group in your class can make your class feel unsafe for students who are in the group, and for anxious students who do not want to be in the group.*

Be very careful about forming static ability groups. The gain must far outweigh the costs. Care must be taken to avoid any public shaming in your class to make this work. For example, you don't want to have a time-out corner that has a punishment feeling toward it. Students could see that you routinely use public shame as a control method, and view "the low group" as an extension of this.

So what do to when you give an assessment and five students do not pass? It's fine to pull those students into a group for remediation, just don't make it a permanent group. It should be formed in a flash group manner where you and your students know the group is temporary.

Having a permanent low group in your class can make your class feel unsafe for students who are in the group, and for anxious students who do not want to be in the group.

Once my own first-grade daughter came home from school nearly hysterical because she'd made a mistake in oral reading and was sure that she'd be put into the low group.

I called her teacher, and she said my daughter was fine, and anyway, "*Students don't know which*

group is the low one." At 6 years old, my daughter knew.

Consider this: when you give a student a role to play, they generally play it. If that role is a low student, you've possibly caused more damage to that student than any instructional benefits of having a low group.

It's not just students who are negatively affected by the low group. In a famous study by Rosenthal and Jacobson 50 years ago, elementary teachers were told that the lowest students had the highest learning potential and vice versa. At the end of the study, the lowest students made the greatest gains leading to the conclusion that teacher this study and five decades of follow-up studies have shown that teacher expectations have a powerful effect on student achievement.

> *Be very careful about grouping lower ability students together. The gain must far outweigh the costs.*

I suggest you avoid or eliminate static ability groups. This is not to say, you stop pulling out students who need remediation or extra practice. You just work to make sure that group is not the same each time.

Also, if you do construct a low group, and it turns out they are all of the same gender, race or cultural heritage, you could be in for a lot of criticism for showing prejudice. Avoid any groups like this.

> *If you have a table with just Black students and the rest white, something is wrong.*

Low Group Story

After looking over the assessments, I noticed three students who didn't do well. One was Carl, whose attention problems made him a particularly bad test-taker. He may have mastered the content, but was unable to show this on a paper-pencil test. A second student, Jose, was just learning English, but was smart as a whip, and probably had misunderstood the directions.

Ashley, who was widely regarded by her past teachers as someone with "low cognitive ability", turned in the third poorest student performance using a modified test. She had trouble learning and retaining grade level skills and knowledge. Ashley was on an IEP, but remained in my class most of the day.

All three of these students failed the test, but should I put them all in the same remediation group? They had all likely failed for different reasons. If I had a calm person sit next to Carl as he re-took the test, he'd likely pass. I knew Jose would pass as soon as I helped him understand the directions. I gave Ashley a chance to pass a test modified according to her IEP since it was unlikely that she ever would pass the general education test. Her IEP directed me to alter the test so she could reasonably be able to perform at her level.

> *All three of these students failed the test, but should I put them all in the same remediation group? They had all likely failed for different reasons.*

I'm telling you this so you can be careful about grouping your students for remediation. Certainly offer remediation to struggling students, but be purposeful and selective in your grouping.

6 Alternatives to Low Groups

• *Modify assignments given to academically delayed students so they can remain, as much as possible, with the rest of the class during independent work periods.*

• *Use parent volunteers and peer tutors for extra remediation. You can meet with your low-functioning students and ask who'd they'd like, and wouldn't like, to work with.*

• *Call back ad-hoc groups of students for remediation, but also high functioning students for acceleration. You want to avoid students feeling like it's bad to be pulled back.*

• *Give academically delayed students additional support when they get to a hard spot.*

• *Think about your students' abilities when designing instruction so delayed students can participate in lessons to their highest potential.*

• *Look for or create opportunities for low students to shine academically in your class. I once had a non-reading fourth grader memorize a paragraph in our class novel, and then called on her to "read" aloud to the class. I still tear up thinking of how proud she was after she "read" aloud to her classmates, and how motivated she became to try harder in class.*

Considerations When Working With Groups

So what do you do with the rest of the class when pulling back a small group? Think about this, if you have the rest of the class doing something with very low instructional value, you could be misusing valuable instructional time resulting in a zero net gain for the time.

The best case is you have the class prepared to practice a skill that they need, so they can move on to the next instructional goal. Students should know what to do and expect a correction if they goof off. Be wary of overusing tablets or computers with low-value, but engaging games. For example, practicing math facts could be high value, a word-search would usually be low value.

Weak or low-value activities include: too much screen time, workbook-like pages only loosely connected to learning objectives, sustained reading time where students are allowed to flip through pages instead of actually reading them, or just about any activity where there's no accountability.

An Excuse to Be Tough: The How to Be a Good Teacher Book

Sometimes a student will overtly challenge school or classroom rules. This might be a student who you are trying to establish a positive relationship with. This happened with me when an emotionally volatile student wore gang colors to class.

Be very careful when coming up with a reward system. It should be simple, successful and short. If the benefits are not greater than the costs, it's an ineffective program.

In such cases I use is the *How To Be a Good Teacher Book* kept in a seldom-used closet.

"Gee, I'd let you wear that hat. Really. But the How To Be a Good Teacher Book says we all need to follow school policy. You want me to be a good teacher, right?"

You can also use the existence of the book to pull back mistakes you made earlier. *"Class, remember when I said you didn't need to read the chapter? I just checked my book, and it says we do."* You can shrug and say, *"Sorry, but I'm trying to be the best teacher I can be."*

You transfer blame for your unpopular decisions to the unseen book in the closet. Let your students get mad at the book if you remind them about school dress code polices, gang attire and so forth.

You transfer blame for your unpopular decisions to the unseen book in the closet. Let your students get mad at the book if you remind them about school cell phone, dress code polices, gang attire and so forth. At the same time, you stress that you are the ultimate authority in your classroom, not the book.

Reward Systems

My colleague told me about her great reward system. She gave out Behavior Bucks (BB) to students who were on-task or doing something she felt was right. Before an assembly, she would announce a bonus of $5 BB to each student if the class needed no corrections. At the end of the quarter, kids would bring unwanted toys to "sell" at auction to classmates with BB. She loved it so much, I decided to try it.

I made up my own BB, ran them off and cut them to appropriate sizes. Students seemed to enjoy getting the paper money and things went well until Peter yelled out in panic, *"Someone stole my BB!"* We searched everywhere, but couldn't find his BB money. Later, Peter brought in a wad of paper-pulp he claimed was found in the bottom of his mom's washing machine.

At this time, I also discovered a black market in BB, where students were trading them for lunch box items.

Soon I found myself spending far too much classroom time trying to manage the BB program, and the day we were to auction off unwanted toys took up far too long. It became clear to me that this management system took far more time away from class than it was worth.

> *The best way to make sure your students are successful is to break the project into very small assignments and check to make sure each student is successful on the micro goals.*

Bottom line: be very careful when coming up with a reward system. It should be simple, successful and short. If the benefits are not greater than the costs, it's an ineffective program.

My favorite systems award "points" to students or table groups, but have no actual reward other than bragging rights. If you stood outside my class, you might hear me say, *"Wow! 23 points! No class has gotten that many since 2018! I'm so proud of you!"*

Long-Term Projects - Avoiding Failure

Long-term projects, especially if there's a home component, are fraught with opportunities for failure.

OK. You pass out a packet with all the directions for the term project. Each element has a description and rubric. You display samples of where past students did well and where they fell short. You make sure that everyone gets it. They must bring in the packet on Friday with parents' initials on it. It's due in three weeks. They can bring them in at that time for a big party where you celebrate their success.

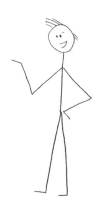

So why the 30% failure rate?

It's because you did not make certain they succeeded.

Everything you did was great, but the missing element is to **ensure success**. The best way to make sure your students are successful on long-term projects is to break the project into very small assignments, a practice often called scaffolding, and check to make sure each student is successful on the micro goals.

What Success Looks Like

Students need to see what success looks like in order to achieve it. Sometimes students come from places where they don't have models of success in their homes or community. If students have no models upon which to build their own success, their path is much harder.

For example, you had them bring in the packet with parents' initials right away.

That's good. Then have them bring in the rough draft of the design for the project to share. Allow students to share with classmates and make changes. At this point, you can see who didn't have a design, so you make sure they have one by the end of the period.

You need to be prepared to have some students complete the entire project in class. One way to do this is to put students who need school support

> *These students have learned to fail. This is not what you want to teach your students.*

into a group to create "*a model for an in-class project*". The students in this group work together and all will have the project ready for the classroom celebration.

If a student fails a long-term project they learn a lesson. The lesson is that they fail at long-term projects. This learning will make it much harder for them to try hard on the next one. These students have learned to fail. This is not what you want to teach your students.

Movement

Moving your students, a least every 20 minutes or more frequently, can have big impacts on

---

5 Teacher Actions to

Make a Class Feel Safe

1. Teach cooperative skills: like how to offer and accept help and advice from a classmate.

2. Immediately put a stop to name calling, teasing or any student behavior that will make students feel unsafe.

3. Model positive reactions to disappointment, frustration and emotional pain. Kids need to see and hear how an emotionally healthy person can apologize, express feelings, and not let set backs interfere with success.

4. Include art, drama, dance, music into your curriculum as you are able. Not just gluing macaroni onto a can and painting it, but teach about line, shapes, shading, composition and so forth — as you are able.

5. Smile, laugh, and giggle with your students. Joyfully celebrate successes with them. A well-managed class is not a dour place.

attention, learning and feelings of confidence. When a student gets up and moves to another place in the classroom, that student's brain gets a boost of oxygen that can affect focus and processing. If you say something like, "Everyone go to this side of the room if you think *Charlotte's Web* has more description text than our current book." Students can have fun showing and discussing their choices. Adding movement to a lesson can be as quick as saying, "Stand up if you agree with this. Everyone? Ok, you can sit down."

Avoid Creating an Unsafe Class

My first class was unmanageable partly due to the class composition: I was given all the "bad boys". The reason given me was that "these boys needed a male" - an insult to capable non-male teachers. After that experience, I became a strong advocate for constructing balanced classes. You may have already experienced teaching with a purposely-unbalanced class, and are aware of the strain on staff morale and student achievement that this practice causes.

The pattern of purposely unbalancing classes can actually be systemic in places where school-wide ability grouping assigns the most fragile learners into highly impacted classes. Such a class comes

Eight Ways to Add Movement
- *change seats with a classmate*
- *clapping or stomping patterns*
- *mirror a partner or teacher*
- *the wave*
- *singing*
- *using wobble chairs*
- *touching the back wall and returning to seat*

"

Moving your students, a least every 20 minutes or more frequently, can have big impacts on attention, learning and feelings of confidence.

ready-made with limited models, low teacher expectations, and unnecessarily poor academic outcomes. Although this type of homogeneous grouping is likely done with benign intentions, the results typically vary between disappointing and tragic. When interviewing for a job, I always asked how the class lists were decided upon.

I've seen lots of methods to insure the classes are as balanced as possible, but the most successful method has a process similar to this:

> At year's end, teachers make up cards for each of their students.

> On the cards are categories that include check boxes for: behavior problem, low, med, high academic achievement, IEP, time-consuming parent, gifted, separate from _____, group with _____. And any other items that should be included based on the students and school.

> Once the individual teachers have made up their card stacks, the teachers come together to make certain the new classes are balanced. Throughout the process, no teacher's names are assigned to the groups. This mitigates stacking a class.

> Shame on any principals who rearrange these carefully constructed groups without consulting the teachers who made them up. Teachers should invite their principal to these meetings, especially if there's a very sensitive classroom assignment.

3

The Safe Student

Topics Addressed in this Chapter

Stressed Students

Bullying

Certainty of Success/Success Therapy

Response to a Wrong Answer

Busting Someone

Five Guidelines for Seating/Moving Students

Getting Help for Severely Stressed kids

Stealth reinforcement

How to be an unpopular teacher

Five quick ways to make your classroom feel safe

It's hard to emphasize just how destructive bullying can be to a child — both the victim and perpetrator suffer consequences if it isn't stopped. Everything you do to make your classroom a safe place can be undone by unaddressed bullying. Even students who are not directly targeted by a bully, understand that they could be the next victim, and feel pressure to join with the bully.

Bullying might seem like it's just a problem between just the bully and the victim. Often other students are aware of the harassment, and feel pressure to either support the bully or fear that they might be the next victim. If caught early, it might be enough just to address the situation between the bully and victim.

If this is the case, and you just give the bully a consequence, he or she will blame the victim, not you. You may want to explain this to the victim—that you are going to give both the bully and victim the same consequence, but then stealthily withdraw the consequence from the victim. That way the bully will focus anger on your broad shoulders and likely lose interest in the victim. The bully may even form a bond with the victim since they are both united in hot water with their teacher.

> *Everything you do to make your classroom a safe place can be undone by unaddressed bullying.*

There is not enough space in this book to give the proper amount of attention to this topic, so I suggest further study to truly learn how to manage student-on-student bullying.

Example of Whole Class Bully Strategy

It was a sixth grade class with a powerful and destructive "girls group" that used negative social pressure to intimidate and bully the other girls. It seemed that nothing I could do would make the class a safe place, especially for my girls.

A trusted educator suggested I plan an activity that gets kids looking for the good in each other; something like a Scroll Party.

This is how a Scroll Party works. Each student is given a scroll (rolled up tube of paper) and a secret scroll buddy. Each day, they had to notice when their buddy was doing something positive and secretly record the good deed on the scroll. Of course, I urged everyone to demonstrate how kind and helpful he or she was in order to give his or her buddy something to write about. The powerful motivation for authentic participation in this activity was the cupcake party where we'd share the scrolls. It's amazing what kids will do for a cupcake.

Buddies need to be strategically assigned. I gave all the powerful girls, a male

secret buddy because the boys in that class seemed unaware of the intimidation that was going on. As such, they were somewhat immune to that type of bullying.

The scrolls were kept by me and "locked up" in a safe place to be added to the next day. I checked the scrolls daily after the students went home, so they didn't become an instrument of bullying. I made sure everyone would be pleased when they received their scroll.

On the last day we had the party, the scrolls are exchanged and everyone got a cupcake. While they were relaxed and eating, I used the good feelings in the room to help build a positive role for the class to play and urge them to continue noticing how well their classmates behave. I was happy with the improvements in my class after the activity.

This is an example of an activity designed to build a positive culture in your class. Think of other ways you can support your students and build a culture of respect and kindness versus bullying.

> *It seemed that nothing I could do would make the class a safe place, especially for my girls.*

Teacher Actions to Suppress Bullying

Start by telling your students that kids in your class value kindness, a class rule. Then be alert to and stop any bullying. Think about these actions and what you should add to this list.

➤ Observe students at recess and other unstructured times if you suspect bullying.

➤ Teach and reward empathy and kindness. Often bullies view themselves as occupying a dangerous place, so a safe class should be a priority.

➤ Build a team feeling where each team member supports the others. *"You don't put down someone on your own team. You build them up so the whole class is stronger."* OR *"We're the Panthers. We don't harm each other."*

➤ Be aware of bullying behaviors so you can put a stop to it right away: eye rolling, staring, isolating behaviors, excluding behaviors, name calling, taunting and so forth.

➤ Involve parents. Tell them your priority is a safe class, and you want to know if their child feels unsafe.

➤ Assign lunch seats if "*Let's not sit next to Jane*" becomes a bullying tactic and institute a policy that party invitations cannot be passed out at school unless everyone in the class is invited.

➤ Enlist the support of other school staff: administration, counseling, other teachers, bus drivers as well as parents to put a kibosh on bullying behavior. There are environments you can control: your classroom. You need help with the rest of the school.

➤ Review school polices on bullying with students and parents. Clearly explain the consequences and steps parents can take to address bullying and cyber-bullying. When students and parents learn it's expressly forbidden and not just a normal part of growing up, you can get more support.

Certainty of Success/Success Therapy

If you take nothing else from this book, embrace Success Therapy.

You want your students to expect to be successful. Students usually define success as meeting their teachers' expectations. Your students need to know, that if they apply themselves, they will meet your expectations. If you have high expectations, your students will know you think highly of them, but you must lay out an approachable path to success.

> *If you take nothing else from this book, embrace **Success Therapy**.*

Sometime during your teaching career, you will meet students who are so fragile, or who have experienced so much failure, that they have become comfortable with it. They will act up to get to their comfort zone: failure. Fortunately, the brains of children are somewhat plastic and can be re-shaped.

Failure-seeking students may be more common in economically stressed areas likely due to the emotional strains caused by insecure food, shelter, and care.

There are several techniques to support these students. My go-to method is something I call **Success Therapy**. This is where you make certain your target student is successful and that they acknowledge their success. A student does not need to accomplish what the other students can do, but just needs to show progress—sometimes in baby steps. You define success for that student and make sure they attain it.

You also make sure students acknowledge their success. Failure-seeking students may not actually recognize when they are successful, so you confirm that they are aware of what they just accomplished. Ask them to repeat after you, *"I'm doing better with each assignment!"*

Tell the student how to feel about the progress. It's very possible that your failure-seeking students would not know that they should feel proud of experiencing growth and success. Emotionally healthy students feel proud after successfully completing a task—much like you do when you finish organizing your desk or cleaning the kitchen.

It's very possible that your failure-seeking students would not know that they should feel proud of experiencing growth and success.

A conversation between you and your emotionally-stunted student might go like this:

Teacher: Ashley, remember yesterday when you refused to write on your paper? But look – now your name is on it. You are making real progress, and I want you to look at your name on this paper and feel a bit proud of yourself that you are coming along. I bet you can start an answer on one of the problems on this sheet.

[Make sure you have a model answer on the board or a sheet of paper for Ashley to see and copy. When you use language like "start an answer" you make your request seem approachable for Ashley.]

The next day.

Teacher: Ashley, remember yesterday when you got your name on the paper and one of the problems done? You are making so much progress, I'm really pleased. What do you think you can do today? I bet you can get two problems done, and when you do – you'll feel great.

As a teacher, you can define success for Ashley. It won't really matter to her that other students are doing much more. She is making steps toward meeting your expectations and learning how to feel proud of herself.

> *As a teacher, you can define success for Ashley. It won't really matter to her that other students are doing much more.*

Busting Someone

Picture a student's self-esteem as a wall made up of big bricks. When you make a public correction using a student's name, you remove one of these and weaken the wall. Fortunately, most students' brains are in a somewhat flexible state, and it's fairly easy to replace that brick depending on how soft the correction is. Knowing that you are causing some possible harm to a student by calling them out in front of the class, should you do this?

Absolutely. It's necessary to make these public corrections from time to time so the targeted student and the class is reminded of the limits, even though this works against your goal of a safe class.

"Stewart, the class is waiting for you to clear off your desk." If you find you are always correcting the same student, you need to meet with that student to plan a way to avoid all these corrections.

> *It's necessary to make these public corrections from time to time so the targeted student and the class is reminded of the limits, even though this works against your goal of a safe class.*

After you've called out the student, and thus removed a brick from the self-esteem wall, you can replace it in several ways. The easiest is to call out the student's name in a positive reference: *"I like the way Stewart's table is working."* or *"I need the class to put away their pencils, like Stewart has already done."* This puts you in the position as searching for something that Stewart is doing well, instead of trying to catch him doing something that needs correcting.

> *This puts you in the position as searching for something that Stewart is doing well, instead of trying to catch him doing something that needs correcting.*

Sometimes, students are embarrassed by overt teacher praise, so you can come up behind Stewart and whisper, *"I notice you are really trying hard on this assignment. Good job. I don't expect you to be perfect, but to try, and that's exactly what you are doing."*

Five Guidelines for Seating/Moving Students to Boost Achievement and Safety

1.   Avoid seating students with attention problems near other students with the same issues. They can trigger each other and make your classroom harder to manage. If you say, "Pick a partner", it seems your two ADHD students will inevitably find each other. Soon you will be working solely with them to make sure they are successful. Sometimes it's best to put easily distracted students close to the spot where you deliver instruction. Also, be aware of students with a hearing or visual problem, and seat them accordingly.

2.   If you are using table groups (my favorite classroom arrangement), be sure to mix genders and races. If you have a table with just Black students and the rest white, something is wrong. I like to make a new seating chart each month. I rarely let students pick their seat location. A study (Bicard, 2012) found that students were three times more likely to be disruptive if they chose their own seat rather than being assigned one.

3.   Avoid seating struggling students near each other. This gives the class an impression that "that's the dummy table". Also, pooling ignorance might not be the best way to make sure they learn. The exception to this would be to try seating ELL (English Language Learners) together, especially if one is more advanced in English that the other and they speak the same language.

4.   Consider occasionally seating gifted students near someone of similar ability. Sometimes you should make sure very high ability students have non-permanent opportunities to work with others of similar talents. These students should have opportunities to work with all students, but they thrive when stimulated by others like them.

5.   When you observe two or three students distracting each other, it's OK to break up the group in a gentle way. For example, "Hey David. I need a helper. Come and sit next to me as I read this story to the class." OR "Roger. I can tell it's hard for you to see where you are currently sitting. Move over here." Avoid making this move seem like a punishment.

Stealth Reinforcement: Case Study

Slade's name seemed to come up often in the teacher's lunchroom. As he moved from grade to grade, his aggressive and sneaky actions had made life miserable for his classmates and teachers.

Then one fall, I saw his name on my class list. As difficult as he'd been as a fourth grader, how much worse would he be as a fifth grader? I wasn't looking forward to dealing with him and his unresponsive family.

Slade accurately saw himself as a troublemaker. He expected his classmates to be wary around him, and for teachers to frequently show their angry faces. He appeared to be entirely comfortable in this role. My goal for Slade became to help him shape a new role.

To help Slade reshape his self-image, I planned to:

• *Make sure he made both large and incremental steps towards a positive behavior pattern.*

• *Bring this progress to his attention and help him embrace the success as his true self.*

• *Organize the class into a structure that offered few opportunities for Slade to misbehave. This organization was highly structured with few choices for students to make. This was not how I liked to teach, but giving Slade too much rope would allow him to tie up the class and we'd all have a bad year. The whole class was impacted by Slade's problems.*

That year Slade was only absent 4 times, and those days were special. I'll admit, I enjoyed the few days Slade was absent as I could open up class choices.

I knew even Slade couldn't misbehave all the time, so I took to "catching" him being good, and pointing it out to him. He wouldn't want me to overtly say, "*Slade is a good classmate,*" or anything like that. He and I would know that would not be honest. Also, Slade would most likely be embarrassed by overt

> *Avoid seating struggling students near each other. This gives the class an impression that "that's the dummy table".*

public praise, so I had to make my praise honest and stealthy.

I did this in several ways. Sometimes I'd gesture over to his table of classmates when I saw him being productive and announce, "*I like the way the students at this table are working.*" This general comment didn't bother Slade, and it was honest. I tried to do this whenever the group Slade was with deserved the praise. This wasn't always easy.

Another form of stealth praise was when I saw him behaving himself, I would come up behind him, and in a whisper, point out what he was doing well, tell him I was proud of his progress and that he should feel proud.

My praise might go something like this, "*Slade, I notice you are following directions again. When you do this, it makes it easier for your classmates to learn. You should feel good that you can help our class. I'm sure your classmates appreciate it, too.*"

> *I would come up behind him, and in a whisper, point out what he was doing well, tell him I was proud of his progress and that he should feel proud.*

Slade had his best year ever that year. He made robust academic gains and got the fewest behavior referrals of any previous year. My other students were unaware of some of the limits I put on the class, and they developed confidence when working with Slade. He became far less of a social outcast.

However, I don't think I permanently turned him around. We only just made it through the year. Still, I credit his progress in large part, to my efforts at helping him build a new role for himself.

The next summer I went into school early to work in my room and a deep-voiced shaggy-haired teen stuck his head in my window, *"Yo, Mr. Hansen. Still have candy in that cupboard over there?"* Slade asked.

As I went over to get the candy, Slade continued, *"You know, Mr. Hansen, You are the only teacher at this school who liked me."* This admission told me I had been successful in convincing a wary and prickly student, that I liked him.

I gave him a piece of candy and wanted to talk about his first year of middle school, but he took off the moment he got the candy. I never saw him again. Perhaps he stopped by merely for a piece of candy or maybe he wanted to touch a place where he felt safe and successful.

Getting Help for Severely Stressed Kids

Rates of anxiety and depression are sky-high among children due to the Covid pandemic and other causes. Much of this is completely out of control for educators. What can we control?

Perhaps he stopped by merely for a piece of candy or maybe he wanted to touch a place where he felt safe and successful.

"You know, Mr. Hansen, You are the only teacher at this school who liked me."

- Take care of yourself. Kids need a teacher who is capable of modeling positive responses to stress and mental health challenges. To do that, you need to practice self-care and

seek help if it gets beyond your ability to cope.

• Stress can cause significant changes in a child's brain, but these changes can be reversed or mitigated by a safe, caring adult. You can be the anchor in the emotional storms buffeting your students. Make maintaining a safe classroom a high priority.

• You can't do it all. If you notice signs of anxiety and depression in your students that cause you concern, seek help for your students. Get advice from administrators as to how to approach parents and care-givers since you are not likely a qualified legal or medical expert.

10 Ways to Show Your Students You Don't Expect Them to Succeed, or How to Be an Unpopular Teacher

1.   Make it a high priority to get through your whole lesson even if some of your students are not following directions.

When students face no corrections for ignoring directions, they see the teacher as not expecting them to learn and make progress. While skipping directions might seem fun, it brings up the question of why they should follow any directions if adults who are supposed to look after them don't seem to care. A clueless teacher might think the students are learning because all the material has been "covered". However students will learn more from a short, engaging lesson. The goal should not be to cover the material, but to convey high expectations for your students' abilities and respect for the curriculum.

2.   Continue your lesson if only a few students are not following directions, since most are.

If a teacher allows some students to fall short, it is noticed by other students. "This is a class where students can fail" is the message that clearly comes across. This message means that boundaries are squishy. How far can a student dig before hitting bedrock and facing a correction by the teacher? Soon fragile and curious students test the teacher to find out at what point the teacher will make a correction. This is obviously not a safe class. Also, you want to make as hard as possible for a student to fail your expectations. No matter how hard you try, you might run across a student who you can't save.

3.   Assign a task, but don't make sure all students do it.

I watched one of my student teachers deliver a middle school writing assignment, then set a timer to raise motivation. Some students were writing, but others were playing video games on their chrome books or standing in small groups socializing. When the timer rang, there was no accountability. The lesson continued. My student teacher did not ask students to show or turn in their writing, and students who did no writing faced zero consequences. Students learned that assignments can be ignored, and that the teacher didn't really care what they did.

4.   Give a direction like "Bring your attention up front" then start delivering directions while just a few students do not have their attention up front.

Signals are a terrific way of getting students engaged, but if all students do not comply with signals and face no corrections, then students learn to ignore signals and other directions the teacher delivers. Best practice is to 1) Once a signal is given, do not proceed until all students are complying. 2) Practice signals if students are slow to comply, or change or teach new signal.

> *More important than any lesson is that students see that the teacher values what's being taught and holds high expectations.*

5.   When helping a student during an independent work period, turn your back to the class or otherwise do not monitor whole-class behavior.

Shouldn't you give your full attention to the student who needs help?

When students are working independently, the teacher should roam. Roaming helps kids focus because they know that help is nearby and also someone is watching them to help them stay on task. When you stop at a student's desk to offer assistance, your roaming job is not over. Keep you eye wandering over all your other students as you offer help to the one whose desk you paused. Keeping the class focused is more important that helping one student.

6.   Tolerate off task behavior until chaos erupts, then yell at your students.

You should view yelling at kids as a profound mistake on your part. If you do this, it's time to reflect on what triggered your loss of control and figure out how to avoid this in the future. Imagine if your doctor yelled at you for not losing weight. How would you feel? Forgive yourself if you lose control, and vow to sin no more. You are just human, but your job is to be a teacher. This does not mean you are harsh. You can be the sweetest, kindest teacher and still be consistent. If you make your corrections at the very first sign of disobedience, you can be absurdly gentle.

7.   Give second, third, fourth chances, because students will view you as the kindly uncle who slips you an extra cookie.

> *If you make your corrections at the very first sign of disobedience, you can be absurdly gentle.*

The role of *kindly uncle* is far different from *teacher*. Students may initially act happy that directions and boundaries are squishy, but they learn to distrust adults who are inconsistent. Fragile students become anxious. That's not to say you don't flex when you need to, but overall, your students need to trust you.

8.   Use sarcasm and humiliation to manage your most difficult behavior problems in order to get them in line.

If students see that you are mean and unprofessional with some students, it will make them feel unsafe. They will wonder if they'll be next. Best is to deal with difficult students with clear and consistent rules and consequences. When students see you do not permit emotionally destructive behavior in your class, they can relax and focus on learning.

9.   If you notice an assignment or lesson isn't going well, force it through to the end.

> *Keeping the class focused is more important that helping one student.*

Your students don't need to you be perfect. If you stop a faltering lesson and say, "Well I didn't plan this very well," they'll forgive you. I had a student teacher named Lauren try to teach a 5-paragraph essay lesson

It can take years to develop the skills to avoid these 10 mistakes. You start with awareness and move toward competence as you practice your profession. Don't expect instant success.

" *Being loved should not be a goal, but the natural outcome of good teaching.*

in one shot when it should have been eight or ten lessons. I watched her throw out her plan and just focus on the first of the five paragraphs. She was good at assessing whether a lesson was too easy or too hard and adapting it to her class's needs.

10. If you make a mistake, hide it from your students so they won't question your judgment.

Like the above comment about student-teacher-Lauren, it's OK to make a mistake. You can demonstrate to your students how an emotionally healthy person handles disappointment. You don't want your students to see you as incompetent of course, but when it's obvious you've made a mistake, own up to it and soldier on. **They'll love you even if you make mistakes, although being loved should not be a goal, but the natural outcome of good teaching.**

Five Quick Ways to Make Your Classroom Feel Safe

1. It may seem obvious, but put an instant stop to verbal and physical harassment. If you think "names will never hurt me" is good policy, you are making a serious mistake. Name calling can put the brakes on learning like few other destructive forces. In olden days, when boys got into a fight, some adults felt a beneficial outcome was that they'd become friends. What's more likely to happen is students will see that adults who should be caring and protecting them, are tolerant of harassment.

2. Celebrate student work. Published posters are fine for the first day or week of school, but are utterly forgettable and unimportant to students. What

students will remember is when they see their work on the walls. Besides putting work on walls, think of other ways to display, acknowledge and celebrate student work. Care should be taken to avoid embarrassing low-skilled students.

3. Smile and laugh with your students. Misguided educators were known to advise new teachers not to smile in class until Christmas. The belief was that students would get the message that this is a serious class and students were expected to learn. In addition, it was believed that students were less likely to act up in class if the teacher seemed dour and strict. The truth is, a teacher who projects warmth and good humor is much more likely to be trusted by students. Such a teacher can maintain a firm grip on a class and still be human.

> *You want to be the teacher that students will want to please.*

4. You want to be the teacher that students will want to please. To accomplish this, point out what you like, what makes you uncomfortable, how you relate personally to classroom lessons. You are basically letting your students know who you are. Students should see a model of how an emotionally healthy person handles classroom celebrations and disappointments. Avoid unburdening your personal problems on your class as they already have enough on their plates.

5. Show how much you enjoy the class. Work toward making students feel like this is the best class you've ever had. You can name your class. For example, you can call your class the Super Stars, and often point out when they are doing well, pleasing you and acting like true Super Stars. This can help them adopt the identity of a great class.

4
Motivation Strategies

TOPICS ADDRESSED IN THIS CHAPTER

MANAGING LEVEL OF CONCERN

NOVELTY AND ROUTINE

USING SOFT COMPETITION IN YOUR CLASS

INSTEAD OF PUNISHMENT

"TEACHER, WHY DO WE NEED TO DO THIS?"

RAISING PRODUCTIVITY DURING INDEPENDENT WORK PERIODS

WAIT TIME/POPSICLE STICKS

WHY STUDENTS DON'T RAISE THEIR HANDS

> *Not all students have this internal motivation, and some that do, get distracted, fatigued, or lack the confidence to fully apply themselves.*

It is easy to teach students who want to learn out of curiosity, natural interest, and the love of learning. Imagine having a class where students willingly try their hardest to cooperate and engage with your teaching. Students who exhibit this type of healthy, intrinsic motivation make the most progress.

Not all students have this internal motivation, and some that do, get distracted, fatigued, or lack the confidence to fully apply themselves. These students need some external nudging. Read this section to learn how and what extrinsic forces to apply that can allow you to help your students develop the built-in feelings that will maximize their learning.

Students who have experienced profound or repeated failures will likely need external motivation in order to learn they are going to experience success while in your class. Once they become familiar with success, it will be easier for them embrace an expectation they will be academically successful.

A typical, emotionally healthy child loves to learn. If you have a student who does not like to learn, you need to figure out what's causing this and attempt to mitigate the blockage.

> *When you announce how much time is left, it can reactivate or reset a student's attention span.*

Keep in mind, you want to use the softest external nudge that will get the job done. Often the softest nudge is easiest and least distracting of external motivators.

Managing Level of Concern

Picture this; you pass out a paper containing three essay questions about a chapter you just read in class. You tell students that at the end of the period, they will recycle the paper before you see it. How much effort will students apply to the tasks on the paper?

How to motivate your students to do well on any assignment? Raise their level of concern. Here are some serious and not-so-serious ways to raise your students' level of concern.

To Raise the Level of Concern

• Have them put their name on the paper. ➤ *They can't be anonymous.*

• Tell them you expect them to do well on the paper. ➤ *They'll want to please their teacher.*

• Tell them that they want to do well on the paper. ➤ *Many students are unsure of what they want. If you tell them they want to do well, they might just try harder.*

• Show them where they will turn the paper in when done. ➤ *They know you'll look at their paper.*

• Explain that you will allow them to stay after school or use recess to finish. ➤ *This is a veiled threat that you darn well expect them to finish.*

• Make a show of setting a timer to indicate when the paper must be finished. ➤ *A timer can communicate that there's no time to fool around.*

• Display a blank bulletin board where you will post their papers, or other ways of publishing their work. [Care should be taken not to humiliate struggling students.] ➤ *When their work is published, it's visible to the community. This is exciting and yet a bit threatening.*

• Explain that they will be working with a partner to improve their paper. ➤ *Since we have a "safe class" environment, I use this mild form of peer pressure all the time.*

• Look at the clock and announce, "Only 3 more minutes left to finish." ➤ *When you announce how much time is left, it can reactivate or reset a student's attention span.*

• Show them a folder that you plan to use at parent conferences. Explain that the paper will go in the folder. ➤ *Most students will want their parents to be proud of them. You'll need to be careful that you don't make your students feel unsafe.*

• Tell them to imagine that the paper goes on their permanent record. ➤ *This is obviously a bluff, and I only use this in jest.*

• Another technique is to tell them to imagine a variation of these actions that raise their level of concern. *For example, "Pretend that this paper will be posted in front of the school so all students and parents will see it when they enter. You'll want to do a good job so you can be proud of what they see."*

After you have raised their level of concern, students will be far more likely to be interested in how to do the paper correctly. They will listen to the directions. When you show model papers, they will be more attentive and want to know how other students found success with the paper. Just about every aspect of the paper will be of interest to your students.

However, if you make your student too concerned, you will negatively impact the feeling of safety that students need in order to take the academic risks necessary for maximum progress. Be very cautious about raising the level of concern too high. Anxious kids do not learn well. Your goal should be to turn it up just enough to get the job done.

When you sense that individual students, or the class as a whole, are becoming anxious, you need to dial down their concern.

Lower Level of Concern

• Tell students that it's OK if they are not quite finished with the paper, you are going to accept it just the way it is.

• Whisper to singularly anxious students that he or she can have more time if needed.

• Announce that, at this time, you don't expect students to finish, and they are going to be able to have more time later.

• Display a model paper and allow students to change their paper based on what they learn from the model.

• Re-define success: "If you got the first three problems done, then you are doing great."

• Give students another chance: "If you need more time, or would like to start a new paper, we'll have time tomorrow."

• Whisper to a singularly anxious student that their progress so far could count as finished.

• Use soft terms like "jot your prediction", or "scribble out a rough draft" which sounds less intimidating than "write your prediction" "or write your first copy".

You are probably already using some level of concern strategies and perhaps not even aware you are doing it. However, expect yourself to become aware of how concerned your students are about the tasks you assign so they can maximize focus and boost learning.

Novelty and Routine

Children learn most efficiently when the classroom has a set of strong, predictable routines: where to put my paper when done, where the teacher stands when delivering instruction, what will happen if I throw a pencil, and so forth. These routines make the class run smoothly and give students a sense of security.

> *If you make your student too concerned, you will negatively impact the feeling of safety that students need in order to take the academic risks necessary for maximum progress.*

Kids crave and need routines, especially highly stressed children, but kids just as much need novelty. Novelty makes it easier for students to pay attention. So for maximum learning, figure out when you need to change something to help your students pay attention.

For example, I was observing Mrs. Belkin, a science teacher, present a lesson on evaporation, when she suddenly said, "*Oh, I need to turn out the lights to say this next sentence because I want you all to remember it*

> *Children learn most efficiently when the classroom has a set of strong, predictable routines.*

> *You will have outliers who need a personalized goal greater or less than the class goal. This amended goal should be whispered to those students.*

for the test." She turned out the lights and whispered to her rapt audience, *"Repeat after me in a whisper: Evaporation is a cooling process."* At that moment, every student became completely engaged as they whispered.

Then Mrs. Belkin said, *"Stand up and whisper it to the ceiling."* Students smiled as they complied, and no one had forgotten the scientific maxim that she wanted her students to memorize.

As an observer, I imagined I could see that information seeping into all her students' brains. It would come out easily when they took their test on Friday. I doubt that Mrs. Belkin had her student whisper scientific principles every lesson, but I am certain she skillfully used novelty as part of her teaching.

Soft Competition

This is a form of non-destructive competition that can really get kids going. To use soft competition, you could say something like this.

"A typical fourth grader should be able to write a 90 word journal entry in the next 20 minutes. Maybe you can beat that? Or, Springfield School has a class like ours, and they all wrote 90 words or more in 20 minutes. Let's beat that."

You will have outliers who need a personalized goal greater or lesser than the class goal. This amended goal should be whispered to those students.

Using Soft Competition in your Class

 Having students compete for honor or prizes can be a powerful motivator for certain students. I've seen students work amazingly hard to prepare for timed tests and other competitive activities in ways that took me by surprise. I've also seen some emotional meltdowns from students who didn't win.

Just as competition can be a profound motivator, it can also crush fragile students and make your classroom feel unsafe. Your high fliers can take over the class to the point that some students stop participating.

I suggest that you use competition, but think of ways to soften it to avoid the disadvantages. You can soften it by having students compete against themselves. So your academically delayed students can see their scores rise against earlier attempts and feel proud of themselves. Sometimes it's productive to have students graph their progress to see how they improve. Other ways to soften competition is to make the stakes low. If you give a $100 to the winner, there's going to be harder feelings than if you give the winner a sticker.

My personal favorite way to use competition is to set up a straw competitor so the class tries to beat another class in a far away school. "*We've done 35 book reports. Miss Anderson's class in Springfield has done 34. They are starting to catch up. Let's all do another one to really leap ahead of them.*"

> **"**
> *You can have the class practice a mantra for students who don't win that might go something like this, "I didn't win this time, but it was fun playing with my classmates, and I improved my math facts.*

A more experienced teacher next door advised me to reward the whole class when TJ met his goal. That way they would all root for him because they would get candy, too.

Games

Think about this. You want your students to practice memorizing math facts 10 minutes a day for a week. How motivating is it for students to flip flash cards on their desks? If they had a partner helping them, motivation would go way up. If they were engaged in a math game using the facts, motivation (and fun) go way up. Sometimes you can use the powerful motivation of a game to encourage unrelated behaviors. *"If our class does well during the fire drill, we can play a math game afterwards."*

Then you can leverage the motivation students experience with a game, to tell them that if they also practice the game at home, they will find more success when they play the game again at school with partners.

This kind of competition could end up being harder than the soft kind we've talked about. Care should be taken to tell students how good winners and players who don't win (avoid the word *losers*) act to keep the class a safe place.

You can teach winners to say things like, *"Good job, Angelina. Next time you will probably beat me."* and so forth. You can have the class practice a mantra for students who don't win that might go something like this, *"I didn't win this time, but it was fun playing with my classmates, and I improved my math facts."*

If your class shows they can't handle this harder form of competition, you might need to avoid using it.

Reward/Consequence

It was my first time teaching sixth grade and throughout the lesson, some students made a sound like noisy intestinal gas then called out *"Excuse me."*

"OK Class. That's it! One more rude sound, and we lose part of our recess," I said as recess time approached. I hoped with all my might that no one would make another rude sound. I needed a break, and so did my students.

> *I had just made life harder for Tim. This would not help him make positive progress on his impulsivity and social skills.*

Then it happened. Tim made a loud rude sound and called out a sarcastic, *"Excuse me!"* He looked around waiting for a laugh from his classmates.

I said nothing, but looked significantly at Tim and wrote "Time off Recess" on the board. Other students cast dagger looks at Tim and inched their chairs away from him. He failed at an attempt to look smug.

The rude sounds stopped, but the class gave all the blame to Tim for a consequence that was not just Tim's fault.

Tim struggled with managing his ADHD as well as trying to find a way to fit in socially with this class. Perhaps I was successful at getting the annoying sounds stopped, but I had just made life harder for Tim. This would not help him make positive progress on his impulsivity and social skills.

Earlier I had a deal with Tim that would allow him to earn a piece of candy when he controlled his call outs. When he got his reward, he made sure the rest of the class saw him eating his candy.

A more experienced teacher next door advised me to reward the whole class when Tim met his goal. That way they would all root for him because they would get candy, too. I could point out to the class that we all owe Tim a thank you for trying so hard to avoid call outs.

Revealing Student's Problems

Here's what you don't do:

"Class Tim has a learning disability called ADHD. He struggles with impulse control and physical movements. That's why he has special rules."

> " *Some alternatives to having students avoid negative consequences, would be to set a system where students are seeking a reward rather than avoiding a punishment.*

Telling students this can actually put a burden on them and open up Tim for teasing or cause serious problems for you because you publicly shared a private medical diagnosis.

Here's what you do:

> Student: *How come Tim gets to have special things?*
>
> Teacher: *That's between me and Tim.* [End of discussion.]

Also, if I want Tim to make social progress, I should avoid making the whole class feel punished for his mistake, but find a more appropriate consequence for Tim that would not impact his social standing.

No matter how well managed your class is, a student with impulse control problems can present challenges. Trying to find ways to address those challenges while preserving an effective learning environment should be a goal for every effective teacher.

Remain vigilant for rewards/consequences that actually make your class a worse place to learn so you can avoid them.

Instead of a Consequence

Some alternatives to having students avoid negative consequences, would be to set a system where students are seeking a reward rather than avoiding a punishment. For example, after the class has behaved well, you could hold up a jar and drop a handful of marbles into it and say, "Class, you've been doing so well with call outs, that I'm going to add five marbles to this jar at the end of every lesson for continued polite behavior. Once the jar is full, we'll have a class reward!"
At the end of the lesson, you point out, "I had to correct two students for call outs, but we did get three marbles. Next time I bet we can improve that!"

If you have a Tim causing all the call outs, you should just have him on a behavior plan, and not direct class ire at his mistakes. The idea is for the class to learn your expectations and feel good about themselves. If your reward system isn't doing this, you need to fix it.

Examples of the Application of Classroom Wisdom

Picture Olivia sitting in your class as you drone on about verbs. Her family is talking about getting a new dog, and it's pretty much all she can

> *Easy and early success can create a momentum that will carry a student all the way through a lesson, a unit and school year.*

think about. You want Olivia and her classmates to ponder verbs for the duration of the lesson. Is it even possible to pull Olivia away from doggy thoughts?

Overt Action. You ask the class to open their notebooks and make a list of common verbs. This requires action on the part of Olivia. Does she comply? She knows you can clearly see if she pulls out her notebook. So she pushes doggy thoughts away and does this, because she knows you called for overt action and will be roaming the classroom for the next few minutes. Effective teachers roam during independent work time to make sure all students are on task and boost students who need some extra help.

Easy Early Success. Olivia also knows that you always put a few examples in front of the class so students can better understand what you expect. Maybe she copies down the two examples she sees on the board. This easy and early success can create a momentum that will carry a student all the way through a lesson, a unit and school year.

For example, consider the first time you played a video game, did you notice it was designed to give the player early success in order to keep the player going?

> *Effective teachers roam during independent work time to make sure all students are on task and boost students who need some extra help.*

Raising Level of Concern. Then Olivia hears you say, ". . . and I'm going to have you share your list with a partner." Suddenly, this is real pressure to focus. Olivia doesn't know who her partner will be, and she doesn't want to appear inadequate to her classmates. At this point, Olivia finds the mental energy to focus on the task. This powerful motivation for focusing came from the type of grouping his teacher uses: Random Partner Grouping. So Olivia is kept in suspense as to who her partner might be.

How to answer this question: "Teacher, why do we need to do this?" OR 10 Ways to Motivate Students to Engage in Learning

You already know that intrinsic motivation is the gold standard. Your students try hard because they want to learn. It's best if you don't need to offer any type of external motivation, but the reality is some assignments might have an element of tedium, or some other impediment, that will need to be overcome with some external motivation.

Some students lacking internal motivation, are distracted by stress, or are reluctant to try hard for various reasons. So there are times you need to provide external motivation. Here are 10 ways to motivate students to try harder that cost nothing and take up only a tiny amount of instructional time.

1. **Explain to students that the state requires that they learn this**. "It's like a law," you tell them. Many students are motivated when they think their state curriculum guide sets out a requirement that they must obey.

2. **Carrot and stick**: "Next year your teacher will expect you to know this. You want to be a good student and have your teacher proud of you and not be embarrassed when everyone else knows this." You tell them what they want.

3. **Tell students they want to get points.** These points are just for honor, there's no other reward associated with them. 10 points for every idea you come up with on your own. 20 points for every idea can get from your partner 30 points for every idea you can give your partner. A point schedule like this encourages your high fliers to help

struggling students. You can also turn the points into a math lesson by rewarding students with fractions, percentages, exponents and so forth that students will want to add up.

4. **Tell them to imagine an external motivation**. For example, "Pretend there's a rich lady with a big purse standing just outside our door. Imagine she's going to give each student $50 and a new iPhone when they complete this assignment."

5. **They should do it to feel good.** Express confidence and suggest how they will feel. "I know you can do this assignment, and you'll feel so proud when finished." When the assignment is complete, tell them, if they really think about it, that they feel proud of themselves.

6. **They should do the work because they love their family.** Use their love for you or their families: "Do this for the class and for me." or "Do this for your family."

7. **Explain to your class that they need to learn to support their friends**. Use students' need to please their peers. "Your classmates are depending on you to complete this assignment." Afterwards, make sure you tell them that they are proud of their classmates, and their classmates are feeling proud of them. This one works best with upper elementary and beyond.

8. **Do it because it's interesting.** Use engaging

content. Use elements from popular culture to make an assignment more compelling. For example, use a Disney theme for a math lesson.

9. **Remind them of their role**: Students in this class want to learn. "You are in this class, and you want to learn. Here's how you do that."

10. **Promise a soft reward.** After we finish this, I'm going to show you how to make a coin disappear. Or, "I'm going to draw three names to lead the line to the cafeteria."

Raising Productivity During Independent Work Periods

Some teachers might assign independent work, then go to work correcting the huge stack of papers on their desk. Once you tell students to work independently, your main job is to roam the room to make sure all students understand what they should be doing and are doing the work you assigned. Don't sit at your desk and correct.

For example, if you tell students it's time for independent reading, you must make sure they are all reading. If you don't, you are actually teaching them to disobey. If you don't plan on making sure your students are reading, you should change your directions to, "*Some of you may read now, others may quietly socialize or draw.*"

If you've instructed your students to independently read, when you find a student who's not reading, use the softest corrections first. If you smile sweetly and point to her book, you've just let her know you are watching and expect her to follow directions. Sometimes I'll sit down next to the student, and read aloud to her as she follows. Then back away. If her book is just not right, I'll drop a few better choices on their desk.

If you put your finger to your lips to signal a student who's talking out of turn, that's a less harsh correction that telling the student to follow directions. If the non-verbal correction doesn't work, ask a question. If you say Jimmy, "*Is our 5 minutes of quiet time up yet?*" That's less harsh than "*Jimmy, quiet down*".

Wait Time/Popsicle Sticks

Effective teachers ask questions that spur critical thinking, foster curiosity, and motivate students to solve problems. Questions are essential for a teacher to get students to process and learn information and skills. It's also possible for a teacher to completely destroy the effectiveness of their questions.

Think about this ineffective use of wait time. Mr. Ishi points to a problem that involves figuring out the area of a right triangle and says, "*Raise your hand when you think you know the answer to this new problem.*"

> *The important thing is to keep all your students engaged in the lesson by training them that you expect them to think about your questions and attempt to answer them.*

The class becomes quiet as students begin working on the problem, then Simone raises her hand and in a flash, Ishi calls on her. The moment he does calls on a student, the rest of the class stops working on the problem. If he had let a squirrel loose in the class, he could not have turned off his students' brains any quicker. A common rookie mistake is to under-utilize wait time.

Here's the same situation, but with different results. Mr. Ishi holds up a cup of popsicle sticks with his students' names on them. He makes a show of drawing one out, not looking at it, then placing the stick in his front shirt pocket and says, *"I want you to imagine that this stick has your name on it. I'm going to call on this student to answer my next question."* Now—do you think he has every-one's' attention?

He asks the question about the area of the triangle, and pauses. Simone's hand shoots up, and he smiles at her silently acknowledging her promptness, but he doesn't call on her. Instead he waits—allowing his students to process the problem.

He waits long enough to determine if all, or nearly all, students have had adequate time to work on the problem. Many hands should be up. If not, he probably asked a question they were not properly prepared to answer. He could give hints or amend the question until nearly all students have their hands up. By now, his class is very curious about the answer.

He waits long enough to determine if all, or near-ly all, students have had adequate time to work on the problem.

Wait time:

The pause between asking a question and calling on a student to give an answer.

Then Mr. Ishi has a decision. If he's unsure if everyone has the right answer, he doesn't want to embarrass a student by calling on someone with the wrong answer, so he can do several things.

Look at the stick, call on Simone (or someone he's nearly positive has the right answer), and then toss it back into the cup before anyone can check to see whose name is on it.

Have students jot their answer on a sheet as he roams the class. He can tell right away who gets the idea just a quick glance at their papers.

Tell students that he will call out the name on the stick, but first they are to compare their answer with students around them to see what others think.

After the answer is out there, Ishi can determine his next step in the lesson: move on, discuss the various ways the problem could be solved, go back and review previous lessons and so forth.

The important thing is to keep all your students engaged in the lesson by training them that you expect them to think about your questions and attempt to answer them. Soon, they will do this automatically whenever you begin a lesson.

Using wait time is an absolutely essential teacher behavior that you need to use with nearly every question you ask your students. Sometimes you'll need to raise their level of concern by applying pressure with a popsicle stick or other motivational method.

> "*If your students don't raise their hands when you use the Raise-your-hand call to engage, you need to figure out why this is happening and find a solution to the problem.*

Why Students Don't Raise Their Hands

If your students don't raise their hands when you use the Raise-your-hand call to engage, you need to figure out why this is happening and find a solution to the problem. Here are some of the most common reasons for a poor response from students.

› **Problem:** Students don't have the knowledge to determine the right answer.

Solution: Give them more information and ask again.

› **Problem:** Students are timid or unsure of their knowledge.

Solution: Give them time to find out what classmates think the answer is and ask the question again.

› **Problem:** They feel unsafe. They wonder if classmates will tease them.

Solution: Take a long look at your class culture and see if you need to make adjustments.

› **Problem:** They are not used to responding this way. Maybe they come from a place where call-outs were the rule.

Solution: Tell them the answer to the question, and then ask them to raise their hand if they know. Make sure everyone has a hand up. Explain that this is how they should respond in your class if they think they know the answer.

This last part might go something like this.

Teacher: Raise your hand when you think you know the answer. [Waits, but few hands go up.]

Teacher: OK, the answer is 8. Now raise your hand when you think you know the answer. Nearly all hands go up—the answer is 8. They all know this. Some might still not raise their hands. Students whose hands are not up, are told directly to raise their hands.

Teacher: Let's look at why the answer is 8, then I'm going to show you a similar problem and expect your hand to go up."

TOPICS ADDRESSED IN THIS CHAPTER

5

Motivating Activities

Create Authentic Projects

You have a darling student named Alyssa. Which of these two writing projects will engage her more?

1. An essay on animal rights, using the five-paragraph form. This will be created, corrected and scored using the state writing rubric.

2. A letter to the editor on adopting orphan pets, using persuasive writing techniques developed in class by studying effective and ineffective persuasive letters to the editor.

In my class, when the local paper printed Alyssa's letter, another letter writer wrote in the following week to say she was moved by Alyssa's letter and adopted a rescue dog. Alyssa and many of her classmates knowing that Alyssa actually saved the life of a little dog shed tears of joy! Such power in persuasive writing!

Look for ways to increase the authenticity of your assignments so students become more engaged and motivated. One of the easiest ways to do this is to "publish" the students' work. This can take the form of posting student work on the wall, printing and binding student work into a class book, putting up student work on the class website or other ways to make their work public.

Awards/External Rewards

"If you reward a student for something they already want to do, you actually reduce their natural motivation for doing that thing." My educational psychology professor explained that rewarding children for something they like to do, replaces intrinsic motivation with extrinsic motivation—not good. We want our students to show certain behaviors because they want to behave that way, versus behaving because they expect an outside reward.

This presents a problem, should the class get points for a whole-class reward for being good listeners, behaving politely, turning in their work on time, keeping their work area tidy? If we reward students for doing those things, won't they lose interest when the reward, and thus motivation, is withdrawn?

It's possible. But you may have helped your students to develop good habits that will take them successfully through the year.

One way to think about providing whole-class reward systems like points, tickets, marbles in a jar and so forth, is to help students become aware of their behavior. Once they are aware, they can modify their behavior. Care should be taken to transition students from the extrinsic reward of points or marbles, to the intrinsic reward of feeling proud of themselves when they accomplish a goal.

> *Use the power of external motivation to move your students to a place they didn't know they could go.*

To help them make this transition, you can suggest to students how they will feel as they make progress toward their reward.

"Yesterday, after the class left, I only had to pick up 5 pieces of trash and put up two chairs. You all are getting to be so good at clean-up. I want you to look around the class and feel proud of yourself and your classmates. I just love this class!"

Ink Pad and Stamp

I was teaching seventh grade language arts, and trying to get students to put the proper heading on their papers. I had an ink pad and stamp and explained they needed their properly-headed paper stamped to get out of the class at the end of the period.

> " *Care should be taken to transition students from the extrinsic reward of points or marbles, to the intrinsic reward of feeling proud of themselves when they accomplish a goal.*

While students were working independently, I could roam around the class and stamp papers. Students were diligent about getting my attention, and I found that I had looked at every single student's paper and had a great idea of the progress of the class and who needed extra help after just a few minutes. I continued using the ink pad/stamp long after my students mastered their headings just so I would be certain to touch bases with each student.

After the heading was no longer an issue, I offered the stamp when students used a quote with proper quotation marks, or some other desired outcome. This type of reward is cheap, effective and will increase the likelihood that you'll touch bases with each student during the period.

Three Reasons to Give Awards

1.   When you give an award, it can create and reward student interest. If your students work toward getting an award, you are using external motivation that you can later transition to intrinsic motivation.

2.   Use the power of external motivation to move your students to a place they didn't know they could go. Maybe a young student didn't realize she could read a chapter book until she decided to get the award. An award can also focus interest where you want to direct it. Maybe you'll give an award sticker on papers with the correct heading. Many students never really thought about the heading on their papers.

3.   An award can create a sense of pride and confidence in your students. You can tell students that their award should make them feel proud and confident, and that it proves they know how to be a good student. And that you feel proud of your class when you see the awards.

The Trouble with Awards

Awards can cause problems, too. For example, a highly motivated student may get every award and spur jealousy among other students. You can head off jealousy when a capable, ambitious student gets yet another award by telling students how to feel about it. For example, you can say something like, "The students at Springfield School got a total of 9 awards, but thanks to the hard work of Priscilla, our school has 15 awards. A school record! I want you to feel a bit sad for the kids at Springfield because their record was broken, but I want you to feel pride that we have Priscilla on our side and in our class."

You don't want to buy a student a pony if she turns in her work on time.

You want to provide the least intrusive and most effective reward possible. Your awards should be modest.

Time Limits

Imagine: you are starting a new unit on weather, and you want to gage your students' background knowledge. You put two weather terms on the board: *clouds*, and *temperature*. These examples will get them started and make certain that every student has at least some words on their list.

"OK Second Graders, you have three minutes to write down every word you can think of related to weather. Begin!"

Then, like a good teacher, you roam around the class to see how they are doing. What if no one knows much at all about weather? They all could be done in 30 seconds. Do you wait all three of the minutes if they don't need the time? How about the opposite? What if after three minutes, nearly all the students are piling on word after word about the weather? Do you stop them while they are so positively engaged?

> *Don't let the time limit boss you. Shorten or lengthen the time to get the most out of your students.*

Use time limits to raise the level of concern, but you are the boss of time. Don't let the time limit boss you. Shorten or lengthen the time to get the most out of your students.

The Power of Mini Lessons

Why do companies spend millions on very short Super Bowl commercials? Because they work. Students, as well as football fans, respond to quick, punchy lessons that last just a few minutes. Look at your schedule to

> *Students, as well as football fans, respond to quick, punchy lessons that last just a few minutes.*

see if you have a 5 or 10 minute slot where you can put in regular brief lessons on a single topic or theme. These small time slots often can be found between lessons, before and after specials like P.E., or around breaks like recess and lunch.

> "If your goal is to help students learn or change a behavior, role playing is the gold standard.

My schedule worked well for a brief, daily lesson on writing conventions. We studied conventional use of punctuation, sentence structure and word choices every day for the entire school year by discussing and correcting a non-punctuated sentence each day.

Role Playing

Have you ever watched young children pretend? They can imagine themselves as a superhero or royal personage and play these roles repeatedly. They often act out a story or video they are familiar with. It's the most basic type of learning and children come to it naturally.

What if you could use this innate need to play a role to help students learn? If your goal is to help students learn or change a behavior, role playing is the gold standard. For example, if you have a health lesson where students practice refusal skills, just telling them to say no when offered mischief, will not likely lead to behavior changes. But forming groups of students to practice these refusal skills can help them build a "muscle memory" so they tend to automatically refuse the mischief instead of having to ponder it and think back to what their teacher said.

With subjects like literature or history, giving students roles and minimal props can compel them to want to truly understand what role they are to play so they will be successful at it. They want to learn the history lesson. You can also watch their role play to see what they do and do not understand about your history or literature unit as an assessment.

If students are unfamiliar with this teaching technique, it's often useful to choose some reliable students to demonstrate to the class what you expect. This can help you avoid overly silly role plays. You can add motivation to the activity by saying you'll pick one or two groups to act out their plays in front of the class. While these chosen plays are in progress, you can "freeze" them and discuss the historical merits of their play and tell students to act out their plays at home for their parents.

The Rookie Teacher and the Master

Part of my current job involves observing aspiring teachers present lessons to their students. For a long while, it confused me when I watched their behavior during independent work periods. The typical newbie teacher will pause at a student's desk to offer support and be apparently oblivious to several off-task students across the room. In conversations afterwards, these novice teachers ask me how it's possible to focus on a lesson and simultaneously watch the class. My answer usually is that the class behavior is more important than the lesson, and that the ability to monitor both will come with experience. A recent study (Stahnke. 2021) of novice and experienced teachers showed that inexperienced teachers were less likely to notice disruptive events in the classroom, and that experienced teachers were more likely to adjust the learning environment than to discipline individual students. Some skills just take time to develop.

6

Effective Daily Practices

There are specific behaviors you can do as a teacher to create a well-managed classroom. In a way, everything up until now has also been about what you can do, but here we look at high-level goals for you to embrace as well as explore the gritty day-to-day actions you can use.

Dominance

Teachers can show dominance in the same way a drill sergeant dominates a cowering recruit, or the way an inspiring leader stirs the hearts of her followers. Only one of these styles contributes to a well-managed class-room.

Researcher Robert Marzano wrote about effective teachers who show the appropriate level of dominance. Not dominance in the drill sergeant sense, but true compassionate leadership where the teacher clearly lays out understandable purpose and guidance in academics and behavior.

True compassionate leadership is the difference between a rigid authoritarian teaching style largely based on intimidation, and a style based on an **authoritative** expectation that students will behave in order to learn.

The opposite of appropriate dominance, is timidity and a hesitant, uncertain approach to leadership. You exhibit concern that students will fail or misbehave. If you can't help yourself from feeling this way, which is how I started teaching, I suggest you work hard not to show it.

Calling the Class to Attention

When my friend was training her police dog, she always started a training session by putting on its halter and K9 flaps. Anyone seeing these flaps, well-marked with the police K9 logo and titles, would know this is a working dog. More importantly, the dog knew it was about to go to work.

> "
> *If your calls to attention are not working, figure out why and modify.*

Children are far more complex than dogs, but a similar idea can help them learn and you to effectively deliver instruction. You instill an expectation for your students that they are about to learn.

When you are about to begin delivering instruction, start by standing in the location where you typically begin instruction. This is your teaching, or power, spot. To your students, this is like strapping on their "you are about to learn halter." For most teachers, their teaching spot is the front of the class near the main whiteboard or projector.

> ▸ *Give your "attention please" signal that you use prior to addressing the class. Orally reinforce the signal with something like, "It looks like everyone remembered to sit down and clear desks." If all students aren't ready, try moving to some of these:*

> ▸ *Identify models: I like the way Bronwyn's table is listening. Continue pointing out compliant students as needed.*

➤ *Use non-verbal signals to laggards.*

➤ *Redirect persistent laggards with a general re-directive comment like, "We just need one more person to sit down."*

➤ *If time and space permits, use a whispered, "Hey Samantha, what are you supposed to be doing now?"*

➤ *If the class is ready and Samantha is across the room, you'll need to re-direct her in front of the class, and promise yourself to give her some positive comments later.*

> **Your voice is the quickest, handiest way to get and keep your students' attention and add novelty to your lesson. Novelty can cause a spike in focus for your students.**

"Samantha? What should you be doing now?

"Sitting down?"

"Yep. Show me you can do that."

All this needs to be done quickly so the students who first came to order don't lose their attention.

If the class is super slow, then practice. Have them all put a book on their desk and pretend to read, then give the attention signal. When they respond quickly, praise them and explain you like it when they are quick to prepare to learn.

Keeping Your Class's Attention: Your Voice

Nearly all the time, you use your normal speaking voice when addressing your class. But soon this perfectly fine normal voice becomes wallpaper and can be easily ignored. To add novelty to your voice, consider changing your voice to a whisper, an affected accent, changing the rate and cadence, adding repetition and so forth. You can hold a cup to your cheek to add a slight echo.

Do not ever yell, but sometimes turn up the volume.

Your voice is the quickest, handiest way to get and keep your students' attention and add novelty to your lesson. Novelty can cause a spike in focus for your students. So think about this when you see students' attention drifting off.

> All this needs to be done quickly so the students who first came to order don't lose their attention.

To boost your students' ability to listen to your directions, you can also whisper. It can be more effective than a shout. Your whisper is most effective when it's accompanied by a forward lean (to show intimacy) and the volume must be loud enough to be heard in the back of the room. It's really a stage whisper.

Like any technique you use to boost your students' attention, it slowly looses its effectiveness the more you use it. Therefore, save it for critical information. Your students will soon learn that they'd better pay attention when you lower your voice. Try this next time you are addressing your class.

> It's more important that you get and keep your students' attention than get through your lesson.

I'm a big fan of voice amplification systems. These allow your voice modifications to carry through the class. Such a system allows you to raise the volume of your speaking without yelling, or to make a whisper easy for everyone to hear. If you have one of these, be sure to turn it off sometimes to add another dimension of novelty.

Most Common Significant Error by Rookie Teachers

I'm not quoting a study from a peer-reviewed journal here, but from my observations in hundreds of classrooms; the most common mistake made by new teachers is to continue a lesson when students are not following directions or paying attention. If you make this mistake, you are teaching your students that, in your class, it's OK not to follow directions or pay attention.

It's more important that you get and keep your students' attention than get through your lesson. It's OK if they learn just some of the lesson.

The Question - A Call to Engagement

OK, imagine this. You are teaching a second grade science unit on birds and wondering if anyone is actually listening. What if you could get your students to become intensely interested in the topic? Just think of how much more they could learn and retain! Use questions to get your students to engage in your topic.

The best questions supporting student engagement are those that lead students to categorize, prioritize, compare/contrast and predict. They compel students to interact with what they are learning. As you teach, see if you can find other ways for your students to interact with new knowledge.

As you look over the examples below, notice how they would require students to think deeply about the subject and perhaps want to learn more in order to answer the question.

> ❝ *It's possible for a teacher to completely destroy the effectiveness of their questions.*

Categorize: We've talked about the various kinds of beaks that birds have. Here are 10 different photos of beaks. Arrange these into groups based on their beaks and label the groups. Explain your reasoning.

Prioritize: We've learned about many of the adaptations of birds: feathers, beaks, feet and nesting behavior. Arrange these in order of importance to

> *The best questions supporting student engagement are those that lead students to categorize, prioritize, compare/contrast and predict.*

the survival of birds. Explain your reasoning.

Compare/contrast: *Think about the feeding behaviors of the humming bird and the robin. How are they alike and how are they different?*

Predict: *Look carefully at this picture of a new bird for our study. It's called a woodpecker. What do you think it will eat? Where will it make nests? Which gender will have the brightest feathers? How does its feet help it to survive? Explain your predictions to your partner before we learn more about this fascinating bird.*

One way to draw students in is to announce that you will give "the right answer" to your question after the class agrees on an answer. Let's say the class decides that feathers are the most important adaptation for survival. You give them an obviously wrong answer to the question and let them "convince" you otherwise. This compels them to dig deep into their knowledge to *"help the teacher understand their reasoning."*

Effective Questions

It turns out, not only are your questions the key to getting your students engaged in your lesson, the way you ask them strongly affects student engagement.

Weak and Ineffective:

Does anyone want to say the answer?

Did everyone understand?

Anyone remember what we learned last week?

Strong and Effective (If followed by a pause to allow them to think about your question.):

> *Raise your hand when you are ready to share your answer. (pause)*

> *Raise your hand when you've decided if you agree with this answer. (pause)*

> *Raise your hand when you are ready to tell me what we learned last week. (pause)*

It's OK to change your directions if you see your original rules aren't working for your students or if you capture a precious teachable moment that needs to be exploited.

A soft call to engagement, like the examples under Weak and Ineffective, are profoundly easy for students to ignore. If Jorie wanted to face the front of the class and think about something besides the lesson, the teacher would never know she was unengaged.

Let's say her sixth birthday party distracts Jorie. It's hard for her to think about anything else. If you ask a question that allows her to stay with the distraction instead of engaging with the lesson, she will not learn as much.

Another problem with the soft calls is that students may not be sure how to respond. Are they to call out? Raise their hand? Wait to be called on?

The soft calls do have a place in your toolbox. If you have a question that you don't want students to feel they must reply to, then use the soft question. An example: Anyone here willing to talk about a time you were afraid?

Effective Directions

Think about the directions you give your class. If you say *No talking*, when would it be OK for them to talk? Should they wait until you are busy, then talk? That's how they got out of control in the first place. Don't tell them *No talking* unless they know when they can begin talking.

Is it reasonable to expect a class full of sociable children to work quietly for 45 minutes? Some teachers tell the class something like this, "You need to work quietly for the next 5 minutes, then only use quiet voices so you don't disturb the other students working nearby." Pay attention to the clock and your students, and redirect any student who talks too soon.

I had done just that, when a rare Sacramento snowfall suddenly appeared outside our windows. Since I would have been unable to stop them from looking out the window at the rare and beautiful snowflakes, I changed the directions to, "Let's look at the snow for a few minutes. Be ready to tell me what you notice."

They followed my directions and dutifully looked at the extraordinary magic of the snow. Since snow in Sacramento likely had never fallen in the lifetimes of my students, I told them to put down their pencils and go out and play in it. To this day, their intense joy rings happily in my mind.

> *Don't tell them No talking unless they know when they can begin talking.*

It's OK to change your directions if you see your original rules aren't working for your students or if you capture a precious teachable moment that needs to be exploited.

Some teachers make directions that are impossible to

supervise. When you do this, you can be inadvertently training your students to only behave when you are watching. For example, if you tell a student to walk to the office on an errand, will you know if they run? If you told them to walk and they run, they will now have experience in disobeying you. Not good.

So change your directions to "It would make me happy if you walked all the way to the office." That way, if they run, they are not being disobedient, just not pleasing their teacher. Not great, but they aren't becoming comfortable with disobedience.

> " When you "think out loud" students will actually copy your thinking processes when they find themselves alone with a similar problem.

Modeling Techniques

I was making an observation in a rough, high-poverty high school. A tiny redheaded woman named Mrs. Alverez taught the freshman English class. Before the bell rang, I'm guessing there were about 40 freshmen students milling about, many of whom looked like adults, and some of whom looked like sixth graders. It was such a beautiful day, I wondered how the teacher would get and keep their attention.

A raucous bell rang just outside the room, and Mrs. Alverez raised her voice just barely loud enough to carry over most of the social hubbub in the crowded classroom. "Find your seat everybody."

I wondered if any of the students had heard or would follow her directions. Mrs. Alverez then pointed at a table where several students had seated themselves, "Whoa! I like the way Jane's table is sitting." The moment she said this, about 60% of her students sat. "Look at Lucien's table," she called

out as she gestured. Nearly all the students found their seats after she said this.

"Yo—Mrs. Alverez. What about our table?" a large girl said. Mrs. Alverez smiled at her, "I love this table Ashley. Good job."

Mrs. Alverez put her finger to her lips signaling the class should quiet, and spoke in a soft voice that carried in the quiet room as students leaned forward to hear better, "I can hardly wait to see what you do with today's lesson."

As I looked over the students, all focused on Mrs. Alverez, I wished she could have been cloned. Her students were behaving because they wanted to. They wanted to please Mrs. Alverez, and they wanted to find out what they would learn that day. They knew she would never waste their time.

Using students as models can help other students understand and follow behavioral directions, but teachers like first grade teacher, Mrs. Jackson, can also use modeling to teach classroom procedures and academic processes.

Mrs. Jackson asked two students to model how to line up for a fire drill before asking the class to do it. As the class observed the model children in their two-person line, Mrs. Jackson told her students to plan out how they will get in line. Having her students visualize their own behavior yields good results.

Later Mrs. Jackson used a different modeling technique to teach her students how to think. She made a show out of pondering a math problem and explained how she thought about the problem.

When you "think out loud" students will actually copy your thinking processes when they find themselves alone with a similar problem. You can overtly tell them to copy your thinking processes when you first use this technique. Later, students will just do this naturally.

Mrs. Jackson: When I look at this problem I see some numbers [She writes the numbers over on the side.] and I see the words Find the difference. I remember that finding the difference means to subtract. I'll put the larger number on top and follow the subtraction process we learned yesterday."

"Now watch me as I do this to make sure I do this right [you ask them to watch you — you are giving them a task beyond just observation as you work on the problem.]

> *If you have a small task on their desks while greeting students, you need to show students that you value this task by taking some class time to discuss, correct, examine or otherwise show that you value the assignment.*

After *Mrs. Jackson* completes the problem, she looks proudly at her students, "*Raise your hand after you've decided whether or not I've done this right.*"

Your Feet Can Influence Your Effectiveness

What do your feet have to do with your effectiveness as a teacher? The truth is, where you put your feet has an enormous influence on your success.

The Doorway Greeting

If you put your feet by the door as students enter your classroom, you have a chance to greet each student. Some studies suggest a positive emotional relationship with a child is the most effective element of classroom management.

For fragile children, this relationship will help them exert self-control when in danger of yielding to a negative impulse. This bond can give confidence to

a timid student who desperately needs to take some academic risks in order to move forward.

One way to manage this greeting is to establish a routine whereby students have an independent task to complete each time they enter the class. Maybe there's a question on the board to answer, a worksheet on their desk, or assignments to copy down. This way, you can remain at the door for the greetings and your already-greeted students have something constructive to do.

One note, if you have a small task on their desks while greeting students, you need to show students that you value this task by taking some class time to discuss, correct, examine or otherwise show that you value the assignment. Otherwise, students will lose interest.

Some teachers call these tasks, Brain Warm-Ups—signaling the start of a learning mindset for the students.

Where you put your feet has an enormous influence on your success.

The Power Spot

Teachers may not know it, but they tend to have a place in the class where they deliver information or carry out discussions. Typically this is near the document camera, white board or lectern. When the teacher approaches this power spot, students expect to listen and learn.

Teachers should avoid standing in this spot unless they are delivering information to help keep its integrity. To foster novelty in the your class, you can tell the class that today's discussion will be held in the back on the floor, and students will enjoy the freshness of the venue change.

The Roam

I watched this happen: Mrs. Lee completed her instruction, verified that students knew what to do, and then asked the class to begin their practice. At that point, the elderly teacher could have gone to her desk to take a load off her feet. Instead, she wandered past every student desk making sure students were on task and understood their assignment. She often stooped and whispered encouragement or advice to students throughout the entire practice period. I don't think I've ever seen a more on-task class.

Would this have happened if Mrs. Lee had sat down to correct papers or called a small group back for instruction? Maybe not. Sometimes teachers need to perform small group instruction during class independent time and risk the decay of attention that happens when teachers don't roam. Get a read on your class and allow yourself to make the most effective use of your instructional time.

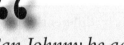

Can Johnny be active while just sitting there at his desk?

Tapping Into a Child's Need To Please

You've been taught that the magic words are *please* and *thank you*. These are indeed effective, but teachers need more than just two magic words. There are certain words that tap deep into a child's brain and, if used, allow a teacher to be more effective. Children can not help themselves from wanting to know what their teachers are thinking.

Contrary to the way many students behave, they are actually hard-wired into wanting to please their mentors. Not only that, but most children have a need to show-off to the mentor. When you use language like, *Demonstrate the correct way to: line up/pick up supplies/share with a partner,* or *Show me you learned how to do a fire drill correctly*. You are tapping into basic needs seated in a child's brain.

Children can't help but want to know what would please or displease their teacher. Some conduct disordered children want to know this so they can do the opposite, but most children just want to know.

When giving directions, use phrases like:

➤ I would like you to . .

➤ It would make me happy if . . .

➤ I want you to . . .

Be open about what you would like to see happen and what might not please you. When a student does something counter to what you asked for, you can use phrases like,

➤ It makes me uncomfortable when . . .

➤ It makes me unhappy when . .

➤ How do you think I feel when I see . . . ?

Using Command Verbs to Activate Student's Brains

You want to keep your students active because it's how they stay engaged in the lesson. Can Johnny be active while just sitting there at his desk?

Think about a student who is daydreaming during a lesson, and one who is engaged and pondering the new knowledge

Some Command Phrases to Use In Lecture

• Imagine this
• Rank these ideas by different criteria.
• Think about
• Now say this in your own words.
• Now compare these
• Picture this
• Predict what will come next
• In your mind, see this
• Visualize a
• Ponder these
• Argue the opposite position
• Arrange these ideas
• Differentiate _____ and _____

coming in. How do you get your students to be engaged while doing nothing but listening? **Covert action.** This is where you keep your students active, but they are not overtly showing it.

Since kids are active creatures inside as well as outside, one way to keep their attention during a lecture is to make sure you, the teacher, control the activity in their brain.

To do this, make your lecture active. Tell your students what to do, think about, draw or write. Use brain-activating directions like: think about, imagine, picture in your mind, compare, remember and so forth. When you give students something mentally active to do, you can keep them engaged in the lesson.

> *Make sure you, the teacher, control the activity in their brain.*

Observing Other Teachers

When I first started teaching, it hit me how isolated I was.
All of us teachers worked in our own classrooms doing our best. Rookie teachers did not have the ability to watch and learn from more experienced teachers. My principal at the time arranged for me to have a substitute teacher and allowed me to observe other teachers who he considered highly skilled. Most of these were in a different school to avoid looking like he was playing favorites.

If you would like to improve your skills this way, and don't have the administrative support I had, you can still gather teaching strategies by observing other teachers. Ask a principal or colleague to teach a lesson in your class, or, with permission, observe specialist teachers. Notice how these teachers solve problems that you have been struggling with. You can also get ideas of what not to do when you see the other educator having less success with certain students and situations. Throughout these pages, I've put in model teachers from whom you can learn.

7

Maintaining a Managed Class

What If Your Class is Out of Control?

If you are looking for authentic, the information in this chapter comes from someone who has had experience in mismanaging a class until it ran out of control and then learning how to bring it back again.

I remember what my first principal told me when I complained to him about my out of control class, "*If Jimmy misbehaves; he needs to learn to manage himself. If the whole class is misbehaving, the teacher needs to learn classroom management.*" Although I've seen exceptions, this is one of those generalizations that is most often true.

As I point out in Chapter 12, I performed badly when trying to manage my first class.

My students were often completely out of control. The only thing that seemed to bring them back was when I yelled over their noise or blocked the door at recess/lunch time until they could become quiet. My class was an unpleasant place. Then I learned how to get them back.

To Get Your Class Under Control

Start Over

My students were noisy and sloppy about following directions because I trained them to be that way. They knew that if I "got mad" and forced them to be quiet, in a few minutes it would be perfectly all right to strike up a conversation that would lead the class to bedlam. The signal for students to start up a conversation is for one student to begin talking and not face a correction.

Simply improving my behavior management resulted in slow, uneven progress. I needed to tell my students that the class will change.

Name It

If you name the set of classroom behaviors you want, your students can understand the change better. For example, tell them a story about a high-functioning class at an imaginary Westgate School. Say, "*Today we are going to do things the Westgate Way for the next lesson.*" Then you explain the Westgate Way is when we work quietly during independent times and raise hands to contribute to a discussion or ask a question.

You, as a teacher learning self-discipline, only need to be an effective manager for one lesson. You can do that. Later, you try the Westgate Way with two lessons and so forth until your whole day is managed for optimal learning. You can tell students that you are learning it as well, so you can use phrases like *Oops. That's not the Westgate Way. Let's try that again.*

You can expand the Westgate Way beyond lessons when you explain, "*Here's how they line up for lunch at Westgate. We're going to start doing that.*"

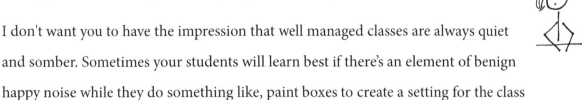

I don't want you to have the impression that well managed classes are always quiet and somber. Sometimes your students will learn best if there's an element of benign happy noise while they do something like, paint boxes to create a setting for the class play. But you want them to understand that you expect them to create benign, happy noise.

Manage Yourself

Your class can never learn a new way of behavior unless you discipline yourself. Be patient as you learn this and feel free to point out to your students that you are learning the Westgate Way as well.

Never Talk Over Students

Delivering content or directions while students are talking is how to train them to ignore you.

To manage yourself, you will need to have your lesson plan either memorized or posted where you don't need to look away from your students.

5 Key behaviors that you must learn to use consistently:

1.   Never talk over your students.

Never. You can't give directions or deliver content while they are talking or not paying attention. The one exception are the Oh-By-The-Way directions (see page 96) given when the class is in purposeful chaos.

Rookie teachers often talk over students. They, like I did, probably figure that since most students appear attentive, it's OK to talk. Delivering content or directions while students are talking is how to train them to ignore you.

2.   Signals

If you teach your students to respond to practiced signals, you can get and keep their attention with very little effort. Teach them some behaviors to do on a signal like *Heads Down, Hide Your Eyes, Clear Your Desk, and Sit On Your Hands*. Other signals like *Echo Clapping, Hands on Your Head if You Can Hear Me*, or playing a music piece to signal clean-up, should also be in your toolkit. These behaviors and signals should be age-appropriate.

Practice and reinforce your signals and realize that each time you use a signal, it loses power. If you do *Echo Clapping* more than once or twice in a 40-minute period, you are over-using it. If students do not respond correctly to a signal, practice it then avoid using it for a while so it can become fresh and effective in a future lesson.

In addition to signals, you can limit distractions and use carefully planned seating arrangements to help students become successful at the Westgate Way.

Make sure each and every student follows your directions or change your directions.

This means you need to be very careful about what you say to your class. Children tend to be literal, so avoid giving behavioral directions like *Clear off your desk, Keep your hands to yourself, Look up at me*—unless you are able to focus on your class and

The Exception: Oh-By-The-Way Directions

Picture this, you given directions for gathering materials for an art project. You have stations in every corner to reduce congestion. You give the signal to begin, but notice your students are basically running from one corner to the other.

Instead of attempting to stop hyper focused, active kids to add to your directions, you just call out: *Be sure to walk between stations.*

You just broke the rule about *Never talking over your students*. This time, it's good classroom management.

make sure they follow those directions until you change them.

3. Follow Through

If you say *Eyes on me*, You don't start instruction until they are all looking at you. You many need to practice the signal, perhaps even multiple times, by telling them to look up at the clock, then restate your *Eyes on me* direction.

4. Soft to Hard Corrections

Use the softest corrections first. If you smile sweetly and put your finger to your lips to signal a student who's talking out of turn, that's a less harsh correction that telling the student to follow directions. If the non-verbal doesn't work, ask a question. If you say, *Jimmy, is our 5 minutes up yet*? That's less harsh than, *Jimmy, quiet down.*

5. Follow Your Own Rules

If you tell your students to raise a hand to ask a question, you can not respond to a called out question. If a student calls out a question, you should ignore it and call on a student whose hand is up or look directly at the student who called out and raise your hand and smile so he knows what you want him to do. If you are not consistent, you are training your students to ignore your directions.

Maintaining Control - Everyday Classroom Management

➤ Make Sure Students Know What To Do When Done

After a student finishes an assignment, there should be clear expectations about what to do next. If the class is noisy, then silent reading is an unrealistic expectation. Some teachers deal with this by having on-going

projects students can work on. For example, a poster or comic strip about a topic the class is discussing. The when-you-are-done activities should be clear prior to students starting their independent practice. Best practice would be to have these written so you can point to the list if a student picks something inappropriate to do. Take care not to overuse screen time.

> *The when-you-are-done activities should be clear prior to students starting their independent practice.*

➤ **Constantly analyze the work you give your students to determine if it's at the correct difficulty level.**

Even the most compliant student will misbehave when the work is too easy or too hard. One way to address this is to have an example up on the board and whisper to your low-ability student that she can copy the example. Have an engaging extension ready for your high-ability students, and allow them to skip unnecessary practice work. Gifted children do not need as much repetition to learn new information.

Avoid giving assignments with short, fill-in-the-blank answers, but instead, provide opportunities for students to write their responses out. Put examples of strong student efforts up in front of the class (after getting permission from the student) to show what you want and what they are capable of doing.

➤ **Limit or remove distractions.**

If you want to keep your students' attention and focus, you will have to limit or remove distractions from them. This can be as simple as

> *Even the most compliant student will misbehave when the work is too easy or too hard.*

*Children tend to be literal, so avoid giving behavioral directions like **Clear off your desk, Keep your hands to yourself, Look up at me**—unless you are able to focus on your class and make sure they follow those directions until you change them.*

telling them to ignore the noise from the class next door, or having them keep their hands to themselves when gathered around the teacher on a carpet.

If you teach them how to start their independent practice with "no talking for the first three minutes, and then quiet whispers can be shared", often students will get so involved in their practice, that they do not start whispering until much later.

To maximize learning, you should teach your class a set of behaviors that will allow you to lessen distractions. This is accomplished with practice, where you give the signal, usually just a verbal explanation: OK, let's do Hide your Eyes.

4 Signals to Limit Distractions

1. Hide Your Eyes

This signal means students put their heads down on their desk with their eyes hidden in the crook of their elbows. This removes all visual

You check for understanding in a way that won't embarrass a student who doesn't understand.

stimuli from students, and should only be used for short amounts of time.

When all students have their eyes hidden, you can deliver

the most critical information of the lesson, you can ask them to imagine something—and since they are in the dark, some students visualize their learning more effectively.

For example, *"Imagine how proud you will feel when you complete this project."* Or, *"In your mind, decide what you are going to do when I give the start signal."*

> *If you want to keep your students' attention and focus, you will have to limit or remove distractions from them.*

Perhaps one of the best uses of *Hide Your Eyes* is that you can perform some formative assessment when you check for understanding in a way that won't embarrass a student who doesn't understand.

For example the teacher has the class examine a problem on the board, then . . .

Teacher: *We're going to do Hide Your Eyes and I'm going to give you three choices.*

One: Raise your thumb if you think the number 8 is too high to be the correct answer.

Two: Raise your thumb if you think the number 8 is too low to be the correct answer.

Three: Raise your thumb if you are not quite sure how to do this problem. OK? Hide your Eyes.

2. Clear Your Desk

It's easy for students to collect items on their desks. Even a pencil and paper can sometimes prevent students from focusing on the lesson. Teach the signal *Clear Your Desk* where the class puts everything that's on their desk under their chair. Then take them through the lesson, which probably involves them looking up at what you are showing them.

3. Sit on Your Hands

When doing a lesson that involves manipulatives, like math, science or art, sometimes you just need their attention for a moment. A child holding a paint brush might have a difficult time looking up at you and examining what you are pointing to.

If you tell your students to sit on their hands, it would be nearly impossible for students who are literately sitting on their hands, to focus on a paint brush as it rests in the paint pot.

4. Close your laptop/put your tablet face down

This one is essential when working with technology.

Re-teach Signals

Using signals to manage your class can result in a profound increase in efficiency. Instead of trying to talk over busy students to explain it's time to clean up and what they need to do, you can teach students to respond to a tone, clap, snap, song or just about any other attention-getting device or noise.

For complex tasks, like cleaning up after an art or science project, you may need to spend classroom time having several students model what "clean up" means. Then you can give the signal and a couple of students model clean up for the class. As they are cleaning up, you can narrate what they are doing.

"Now class, notice how Kenton is showing that we rinse out the paint brushes and put them handle down in the brush container, and Tommy is putting his wet painting on the drying rack after he puts his name on it."

You can go so far as to have students close their eyes and imagine themselves going through the clean up process to help them remember what to do. This works well from kindergarten though high school.

Complex tasks like *clean up* often work better if a list of what you expect students to do is posted. When Kenton tells you he's done, you can ask him to check the list just to make sure.

> " *Complex tasks like **clean up** often work better if a list of what you expect students to do is posted. When Kenton tells you he's done, you can ask him to check the list just to make sure.*

If you use a bell for the clean up signal, it's better if you don't use that bell to signal other tasks, save the bell for clean up and use other signals for other tasks.

Start your activity and when you determine it's time to clean up, give the signal. Praise students who are following procedure.

> " *Signals usually need to be re-taught to maintain their effectiveness.*

Use questions like, *"Kenton? Did you hear the signal?"* to redirect students slow to respond.

For students who need the advance warning, you can whisper to Tommy, *"I'm going to give the clean up signal in one minute. You can start your clean up now before anyone else is back at the sink."*

It will be amazing! While other teachers avoid untidy, but

wonderful activities, your class will fully immerse themselves in powerful, messy learning experiences.

But the next time you have an art project, the signal will likely not work so well. Each time after that, the signal will be less effective. Signal compliance is like an empty kitchen counter top—it gets cluttered over time unless energy is applied.

Signals usually need to be re-taught to maintain their effectiveness. The best way to do this is to make the re-teaching light, quick but serious. For example, you give the signal for "voices off and eyes on me" and only 80% of students comply. If you go ahead and give directions or deliver content with less than 100% of students attending, you are effectively teaching your students to ignore you.

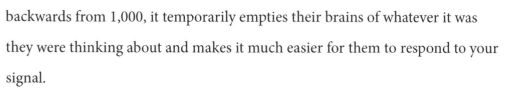

Instead, what you can do is say something like, *"Oops. We are better than this. Let's try that again. Everyone start counting in Spanish."* When you tell them to count in Spanish, or to count backwards from 1,000, it temporarily empties their brains of whatever it was they were thinking about and makes it much easier for them to respond to your signal.

Then you repeat the signal. You should get 100% compliance at this point. Praise them for how well they respond to the signal, and tell them how much you love this class.

I'll Wait

The wiggly kindergartners did not come to attention when Miss Johnson asked for it. She put a determined look on her face and said, *"I'll wait."*

> *When you tell them to count in Spanish, or to count backwards from 1,000, it temporarily empties their brains of whatever it was they were thinking about and makes it much easier for them to respond to your signal.*

It worked! Quickly the voices and wiggles stopped.

If Miss Johnson had tried the *I'll Wait* technique in sixth grade, it could have resulted in a huge loss of instructional time. A sixth grade teacher can effectively use the *I'll Wait* technique when students are in a rush to get to the good part of the lesson. If you are going to give them directions on how to do a boring worksheet, why should they be in a rush to hear about that?

If your calls to attention are not working, figure out why and modify.

How-to-Know-When-You-Are-Done Limit

I had prepared my students for a journal-writing period. We had brainstormed topics, made a list of useful words and studied models. Now it was time for them to write. I made a show of starting a timer and told them they had 20 minutes. Then I rang a bell to show them the time had started.

Call Outs

When a student calls out an answer, the rest of the class stops working on the problem. They learn less.

As I roamed around the room helping and encouraging, I noticed that nearly all the students had filled a page after about 15 minutes, but some very capable students just had a dozen words. I needed to get more out of those unproductive students, but how?

I learned to set how-to-know-when-you-are-done limits. Now I add this to my directions: *"A typical fourth grader can write 90 words or more in 20 minutes. You will know you are done when you get that or more."*

Then I adjust limits for students who cannot get to the how-to-know-when-you-are-done limit. I might whisper to a student, *"Brian, yesterday you wrote 19 words. You are a day older now; you are done when you have twenty words."*

Limiting callouts: Getting the most out of your questions

We've looked *at how important questions are for a teacher to get students to process* and learn information and skills.

It's possible for a teacher to completely destroy the effectiveness of their questions. Here's how it can happen: allowing callouts.

Picture Mr. Madison as he asks the class a question that requires them to think about previously learned knowledge and apply it to a new situation. It's a powerful and complex question. For example, *"Yesterday we learned the six ways to start a non-fiction essay. Look at today's essay example and decide which start the author choose."*

Mr. Madison wants his students to think about previous lessons and apply their knowledge to a new situation..

> ❝ *It's possible for a teacher to completely destroy the effectiveness of their questions.*

Sam yells out, "It's the Story Start! The author begins by telling a story."

As soon as those words leave Sam's lips, the rest of the class stops thinking about the question. Those students won't have made the logical connections to allow them to easily internalize how to apply their knowledge of essay starts to a new essay.

What if Mr. Madison had phrased his question a bit differently?
"Class, raise your hand when you are ready to explain your thinking about my question."

If Mr. Madison has built a classroom routine where there are times when students can call out answers and times when they must raise their hands, his students will learn much more. He uses verbal and non-verbal signals to tell students how to respond to his questions.

I suggest you have a signal for times when you want your students to call out answers. For example, you can ask a question, pause to let students process their answer, then signal that they all respond at once.

The Start Signal

Your students need to know when they should stop looking up at you and then turn their attention to their written work. I find that if I use a Start Signal, it catches the students who were politely looking up at me, but whose minds were somewhere else.

> *A student with attention problems may look at a sheet that's dense with text and feel defeated instantly.*

It works like this, *"Are there any more questions? No? OK. Ready? Begin"* (soft clap) If you follow the word *Begin* with an attention-getting noise, it cuts through the fog of your dreamers and attention-problem students. You'll get a much higher compliance rate with a start signal so students clearly understand that they should begin working inde-

pendently.

One way to practice this is the have your students prepared to begin with pencil poised over paper, but tell them not to start. Wait for the start signal. Once you give the signal, it's easy for you to assess who is on task and who isn't.

Teacher-Made Papers — Graphic + Name

When you make up a paper for your students to use in a learning situation, be sure to put a graphic on it and a fill-in-the-blank place for the student's name and any other information you need to have on that sheet. This blank will greatly increase the possibility that Mary will remember to write her name on the paper.

Another way to get names on papers is to tell the class that they've been working so hard, they should put a tiny star by their name. Students who haven't put their names on the papers will do that in order to get the star.

Why the graphic? A little picture on a worksheet can soften the assignment and make it seem more approachable and less onerous. A student with attention problems may look at a sheet that's dense with text and feel defeated instantly — much like you feel when you see a massively dense email message. The graphic will increase student engagement. You may have noticed I've used graphics and break-out quotes within this book. I want to

> *A student with attention problems may look at a sheet that's dense with text and feel defeated instantly — much like you feel when you see a massively dense email message.*

keep your attention.

I like to use graphics that have something to do with topic being studied, but it's not necessary. One teacher I know bought a collection of cat images. She tells her classes she loves cats, and puts a different cat graphic on every sheet.

A graphic can help students organize their work. For example a teacher could say, "Class, please take out the vocabulary sheet for the second chapter of *A Separate Peace*." Looking through a stack of papers, students might not have any idea of which sheet that is.

But if the teacher says, *"Class, please take out the vocabulary sheet for the second chapter of A Separate Peace. The one with the cat wearing a chef's hat."* The sheet will more likely be located quickly.

Playground, Cafeteria, and Bus Duty

Part of teaching is pulling supervision duty while other staff members get a break. After being in a classroom with a bunch of kids, it will be tempting to find another adult on duty and chat while students enjoy their playground. I would urge to you to avoid the temptation and focus on your charges, unless your students possess the ability to solve conflicts without adult intervention.

Before taking a duty for the first time, find out what the protocols are for minor and major medical emergencies on the playground, what's expected if you find students physically fighting or bullying, and so forth. Once outside, position yourself to eliminate blind spots.

Approach anyone who doesn't belong on the playground and follow school protocols for this situation.

While on duty, here are some of your tasks:

1. Are students playing safely and following school rules?

2. Can you spot any minor conflicts that might escalate? It's far easier to defuse a pair of chest-bumping boys than deal with a fist fight later on.

3. Do you see a group of students gathered in a tight circle? This often means something bad might be happening, so wander over to see what they are doing.

4. Can you find an isolated student and learn if they are just a happy introvert, or need some support to get involved in a game?

5. Can you find a student in distress and figure out how to calm them?

6. Observe your own students to see if you notice something that you want to discuss with them later or bring up at parent conferences.

7. As much as you might crave just a tiny bit of adult conversation, avoid standing next to a colleague unless there are plenty of staff members on duty to cover the area.

Teacher In Front of Whole Class vs. Small Group Considerations

Advantage of Teacher in Front

Teachers can see every single student at once and is much more likely to spot students disengaging from lessons or misbehaving. Steps can be taken instantly to reengage or re-direct students.

Advantage of Small Group

Some students learn best when in close proximity to the teacher. Teachers deliver instruction to a few students and can assess progress, so adjustments can be made for those students. This is especially true of younger students. With small group teaching, the effectiveness depends on what all the other students are doing. If engaged with low-value activities, the small group advantage is greatly diminishes.

8

Everyday Teaching Strategies

Topics Addressed in this Chapter

The title of this book is subtitled, *Classroom Wisdom from a Master Teacher.* To me that means readers can trust the information in this book to take them beyond theory and into the realm of science-based, field-tested actions and attitudes an effective, advanced teacher must embrace. So far, we've looked at many aspects of classroom management. This chapter has direct examples of how to apply these principles to your own teaching. As you read these, think about how you could modify them to fit in with your partic- ular students and school culture.

Winning Power Struggles

If you are in a power struggle with a student and lose, it weakens your position for future confrontations with that student. If you win the struggle, the student may feel humiliated and/or resentful — which can weaken your position for future confrontations with that student. Truly, the only way to win is to never participate in arguments unless it's an academic activity.

> **Never repeat directions. Instead ask questions.**

Some students easily engage their parents and other family members in arguments. They often don't argue to win; it is a form of recreation for them. When they arrive at school, they can be amazingly skillful and eager to see what happens when they try their arguing skills on the grownups in their classrooms. Stay alert for student attempts to pull you into an argument.

If the teacher has an established signal for clean up, a triple hand clap for example, the student can't very well claim he didn't hear it.

This signal works best when established prior to the start of the lesson and used throughout the school year. If you know Sam needs to test adults, prior to the signal you can ask him, "What are you going to do when you hear the signal?"

> **Truly, the only way to win is to never engage in arguments.**

Here's how a conversation might go down with an expert student arguer:

Analysis of Teacher Behavior:

The teacher lost points by repeating the directions. It would be better to ask Sam a question like, "What are you supposed to be doing?" or "Sam, why are all your classmates cleaning up?"

The biggest mistake the teacher made here was responding to Sam's assertion that he "didn't say anything". As soon as the teacher responds to his misstatement, Sam has won. The teacher should have said something like, *"Maybe I didn't say anything, but you still need to clean up."* Teachers should never argue with a student.

The second biggest mistake was when the teacher boxed herself into a corner where she must give a consequence to Sam. Sam has his honor to uphold and may even view himself as a person who should be punished. Several other students are watching this exchange, so Sam can't back down without social consequences. No matter what happens, both the teacher and Sam lose.

The Wrong Way

Teacher: *Time to clean up. Everyone put away your supplies.*

Sam: (Does not put away anything.)

Teacher: *Hey Sam. I announced it's time to clean up.*

Sam: *You didn't say anything.*

Teacher: *Just a few minutes ago, I told you to clean up.*

Sam: *No you didn't.*

Teacher: *I did too. If you don't clean up, you are going to get a behavior slip.*

A Better Way

Teacher: *Who can tell me what to do when you hear the echo-clap?* (Waits for nearly all hands to be raised.) *Angelina?*

Angelina: *It means clean up.*

Teacher: *That's right! Show me how we do clean up.* (Does echo clap.)

Sam: (Does not clean up.)

Teacher: (Stands silently near Sam and does not look at him.)

Sam: (Still does not clean up.)

Teacher: (Apparently noticing Sam for the first time.) *Sam?* (Sounding a bit surprised.) *Hey Sport. What are you supposed to be doing?*

Sam: *I don't know.*

Teacher: *I'd find out if I were you, and get started.* (Teacher turns her back on Sam and appears to pay attention to some students who are following directions.)

By calling on a student to give directions, students get a social reward: a correct oral answer in front of her peers, and it's clear that your directions are understandable.

Students love to show off to the adults in their lives. When the teacher says, *show me*, students cannot help but try to follow directions.

When Sam does not comply, the teacher first uses a non-verbal, proximity reminder to get Sam's attention. Non-verbal cues allow Sam to comply without losing face with his peers.

The teacher feigned surprise that Sam wasn't cleaning up to give him the impression that she has high expectations for him. She is saying, "You are the kind of person who likes to clean up promptly.

This teacher knows Sam has behavior problems and has approached him at times when no conflict issues are present. They've discussed basketball and the teacher calls him *Sport* to remind Sam that they share the basketball connection. It's also a sign of affection that Sam tolerates well.

The teacher does not tell Sam what to do, but instead asks a question. This is another management technique that few rookies do well: *never repeat directions, instead ask questions*. Questions compel the student to think, not just react.

Asking questions instead of giving directions.

If you look at the last teacher behavior, she has not put Sam in a spot where he loses face with his peers if he complies with her. About now, the teacher will execute a brilliant move, turning her back to Sam. This can give him a bit of time to think and start his clean-up without appearing to lose a battle.

Allowing the student to save face.

If Sam still didn't clean up, an effective teacher would give him some choices instead of boxing both the student and the teacher into a place neither want to be. A conversation might go something like this:

Giving Choices to avoid getting boxed in

Teacher: *Well Sam, it looks like you've decided to delay your clean up. You have a choice between starting your clean up right now or coming in during break time to do it. Now make a good choice.* (Then the teacher would turn her back on Sam and engages with another student as if she fully expected Sam to start his clean up.)

Showing high expectations.

In truth, Sam has dozens of choices, but the teacher has limited it to two. One of these is much easier on both parties. By telling Sam he gets to choose, he still has a feeling of power. If he makes a poor choice, the teacher can discuss with him that he lost his free time due to his own choices, not due to the "teacher being mean".

Letting the student keep a feeling of power.

Definition: dead time

This is when your students have nothing to do. Perhaps materials are being passed out, some random kid is doing a problem on the board, or the teacher is performing a demonstration and the student can't see what's happening. Dead time often precedes mischief or disengagement in the lesson.

Making Classroom Demonstrations Work

You've asked a student to do a problem on the white board in front of the class, you've asked a group to perform an experiment in front of the class, or had a pair of students carryout a process for the class. This is where students' attention can start to drift away from your lesson.

As soon as a student begins to write on the board, other students are likely to lose their focus and disengage from the lesson because they have nothing to do. Truly motivated students will pay attention because they are curious, but not all of your students are so interested. These students could and likely will, cast their attention

> *An effective teacher can't allow unengaged students.*

elsewhere. An effective teacher can't allow unengaged students.

Teacher Model: The Demonstration

As part of my job in the Education and Counseling Department of Lewis and Clark College, I observed a veteran teacher, Mr. Garcia, do three things that resulted in effective classroom demonstrations.

1. Mr. Garcia made sure that all students could see the demonstration so he could avoid dead time. If a student is visually cut off from the show, there's no more reason to pay attention to the lesson. I watched Mr. Garcia praise a student who moved to the front of the room and sat on the floor in order to see what was going on. In his class, it's a student's duty to see what's happening, so students are praised for making sure they can see.

Probably of these three steps, the most important was giving everyone in the class something to do when a student approaches the board.

2. Prior to starting the demonstration, he made all students predict what was going to happen. His students had access to scrap paper, and he instructed each student to quickly jot down what they thought the results would be. Mr. Garcia then had students share their prediction with a partner and allowed them to change their predictions after the sharing. By the time the demonstration began, all students were curious to see what would really happen.

3. Just before the demonstration was to begin, Mr. Garcia told his students that he wanted them to watch the demo carefully to see if their predictions were right. This was key; he gave all students a job to do. They must not just sit and watch, but truly pay attention to confirm their ideas.

Probably of these three steps, the most important was step number 3—giving everyone in the class something to do when a student approaches the board. Next time you have a student come to the front to attempt solving a problem, or some other demo, think about Mr. Garcia's technique.

Boosting Quantity: Team Brainstorming

Having students produce a **quantity** of work is a vital part of effective teaching. If you have an emergent reader who struggles through 2 books a day, that student is far more likely to develop reading fluency than a student who reads one book a day. Likewise if you have a class where they have 20 essay ideas versus a class with one essay idea, which class might have students who are successful at finding a motivating essay topic?

Think about this scenario. You finish the class novel and you want your students to remember key connecting points in the book so they can learn the common structures of literature. You put a chart paper up and ask students to raise their hands when they can think of a way the author connected the end of the book to the beginning.

Making Effective Classroom Demonstrations

1. *Make sure students can see.*
2. *Build engagement by having students make predictions.*
3. *Instruct students to carefully watch to check their predictions.*

> " *You want your students to be unfamiliar with academic failure.*

You will always have students who dominate such a scene because they are enthusiastic and smart. Their hands are up, and their answers are good.

You have other students who will contribute with some urging. And you also have students who hang back or don't participate at all. Maybe they are unsure of themselves or have another reason for not engaging. They may be lost in their dream world and not even think about your request.

How can you get 100% of your students to participate? Highly skilled teachers want all students engaged. You want your students to be unfamiliar with academic failure.

Here's a strategy you can apply and adapt to your class: **team brainstorming**. As you read the directions, notice that many classroom management techniques are also used, besides just the brainstorming.

Team Brainstorming: Directions (complete explanation)

You tell your class that when you give the start signal, they will have three minutes to record every connection the author used from the beginning of the book to the end. This gives them a clear goal and time limit. The time limit will raise their level of concern. They have a few items already on the chart paper up front that they can copy in case they can't think of anything themselves. Providing models will raise their chances of success.

> **A Class Discussion**
> Students can see peers excited about the curriculum and that infectious excitement translates to interest and motivation.

You boost external motivation when you tell them they will get one point for every word they write.

You expect everyone to have at least 20 points by the end of the three minutes. This shows your high standards for all students, but you can whisper a different goal for struggling students.

Explain that the record for finding the most connections belongs to a sixth grade class in Springville. That class found 63 connections. You don't expect your fourth graders to get anywhere close to that huge number. This kind of soft competition of a distant class can raise engagement, but keep stress down.

Before giving the start signal, you show the sheet of chart paper and tell them to raise their hand when they can think of a way they can add to the list of connections already started. You wait until most of the class has their hands up.

Call on two or three students and record their answers. Using student models can make the assignment goals seem attainable and help students understand what you are looking for. Your least-able students can copy the answers so they will be working just like their classmates.

You point to the chart paper, "There are already seven words on this chart. If you copy these, you'll just need 13 more points." This makes the goal even more approachable so students will have an expectation of success. This expectation lowers anxiety, but not motivation.

> *You can see how Team Brainstorming engages 100% of students, uses level of concern, external motivation, soft competition, use of models/examples and other prime classroom management techniques.*

Explain that when the time is up, you will assign them a partner with whom they will share their list. This adds social motivation. Students do not want to seem foolish in front of their classmates, so this provides very strong motivation for them to participate.

Hold up a stopwatch, timer or your phone. "Any questions? Ready? Begin!" A soft clap at this point and the timer adds to students' level of concern and boosts motivation.

While they work, you roam around the class. Roaming raises level of concern and comfort because when you roam, students know they can't just skate by, and you will help struggling students be successful.

If a student isn't writing, you tell them to copy the words off the board. You told your class they'd have 3 minutes, but this lesson is not about time, it's about literature. So you give them more time if they are rocking this list, and less time if they seem to be stuck. For this reason, I do not display the timer.

Soon your high fliers will be close to the 63-point "record" and very excited. You show excitement, too. When time is up, give the stop signal. I use, "Stop. Pencils down." Have them add up their points and record it at the top of their paper.

You can explain, that the 63-point record was done with just remembering, but the true amazing record was over 217 points when the class got to look back at the book. Express confidence that they can beat this look-back record.

Give them 20 minutes to re-read the first chapter of the class book and jot any more connections they find. You want them to re-read the first chapter because they just finished the last chapter. It's still fresh in their minds, and when they read the first chapter, they are getting reading practice, but also making connections.

Explain that when they share with a partner, they will get 2 points for every idea on their list that their partner doesn't have, and 5 points for every idea on their partner's list that they don't already have. This encourages students to give and accept connections to build their lists. You want a team spirit taking on that class in Springfield.

When this project is complete, your students will have pulled all the connections from their memory, from re-reading the first chapter, and from working with a partner. They will have blown the Springfield record out of the water, and feel proud of themselves and their class.

I like to collect their lists, edit them and pass out the edited collection so they can paste them into their writing journals.

Did you notice how Team Brainstorming engages 100% of students, uses level of concern, external motivation, soft competition, use of models/examples and other effective classroom management techniques?

Try to think of ways to modify Team Brainstorming to make your class more engaging. Think of ways to keep your students engaged in your instruction.

And the points? Do students get anything for these besides fun? Nope - just bragging rights over that Springfield class. You are off the hook for coming up with a prize. I suggest skipping the whole points part or any other external motivation if your class already is sufficiently engaged.

Critical Learning Opportunities

I was teaching in a school located in an affluent

A Version of Team Brainstorming

1. Present goal and time limit.

2. Get a few items on the chart paper to serve as models.

3. Explain that when time is up, they will share their list with a partner, so both partners can add to their lists.

4. Start the time where students work independently. You roam to check for understanding.

5. When time is up, assign partners and give students time to share with their partners.

6. Have a class discussion where students add to the list on the chart paper. If time permits, have them rank the top 5 items on the list.

area where parents often planned on taking their kids out of school for skiing vacations or amusement park trips. In one of my first newsletters, I tried to stop this by saying that ANY time a student missed school, I could guarantee their child would miss something important.

Parents needed to be taught that doing a worksheet on vacation could in no way replicate the power of an engaging classroom discussion. I never make packets for these parents. I have a standard assignment sheet for students who leave school early: Read daily for 20 minutes, and write 90 words or more in your journal.

Critical Times Before Holidays

Years ago the US Army — probably the institution that trains and tests more students than any other school — did research that showed that recruits best retained the knowledge from the first things learned and the last things learned. As a result, instruction was modified to present the most critical information near the beginning and end of each course.

> *It's true that Winter Break is a stressful time for many children as split families often shuttle kids, and other family routines are broken, but expect your students to learn.*

You will hear teachers say that they can't present new information before winter break because they kids can't focus. Baloney! It's true that this is a stressful time for many children as blended families often shuttle kids and other family routines are broken, but expect your students to learn. During stressful times, children are often comforted by your class leaning more toward routine and less toward novelty. That's not to say you skip important activities like class parties to teach special lessons on gerunds and infinitives.

However, instead of doing something unproductive, like showing a movie that lacks nearly any instructional value, the teachers should be presenting important and engaging content, and expecting students to retain it. Don't waste high impact learning times.

Teacher Model: Mrs. Park - Delivering the Right Re-direction

> *During stressful times, children are often comforted by your class leaning more toward **routine** and less toward **novelty**.*

Mrs. Park began her science lesson. At one point, a wiggly blond boy began making obnoxious noises using the materials. Mrs. Park gave him "the look" and he sheepishly stopped.

Later a slender, curly-haired girl began making nearly the same noises. This time Mrs. Park did not use her look, she continued her teaching, but moved in a comforting way next to Curly Hair. The noise stopped.

At another point in the lesson, Mrs. Park whispered to another noisy boy: *"Charles, that's enough noise right now."*

Three different students making the same error, and yet three different responses.

Watching Mrs. Park, a top educator, work with her third graders never ceased to amaze me. How did she get them to the point where they craved to obey and learn from her? What were her secrets?

The feeling tone in her class was warm and loving, yet business-like. There was lots of fun going on, yet no fooling around. It was so perfect; I wished I could be a student in her room.

I reflected on what she was doing and realized she had four important practices going on to make her class so well managed.

1) Relationships When her students entered the class, she always greeted each student personally—often mentioning something of importance to that child. "*Good morning, Ben. How's your hamster doing?*" The teacher-student relationship is the most profound component of effective classroom management.

When a student misbehaved, Mrs. Park would use her knowledge of that student to decide why that student was acting out and address the cause. It might be the child didn't hear the directions, the child feels uncomfortable, or perhaps a student just needed to be reminded of where the limits were. Since the students felt Mrs. Park understood and cared about them, they accepted and embraced her directions.

2) Safety and Concern Mrs. Park made sure that students felt they could step into unfamiliar waters and take academic risks without fear of ridicule or failure. She also kept as much pressure to perform as possible, without going to the point of causing a meltdown for an anxious student.

3) Organization Students knew what was expected by the routines established during the first week of school and supported by clear, simple directions during projects and instruction. Nearly no instructional time was wasted because students knew how to handle their materials and transitions. I did not witness Mrs. Park doing it, but I'm certain she practiced transitions between activities during the first weeks of school.

4) Difficulty A teacher like Mrs. Park knows her students' abilities and the curriculum. During her instruction, she monitors her students' learning and adjusts the lesson to take full advantage of her observations. A good teacher will often check for understanding and adjust or even abandon a lesson plan when she deems it ineffective.

> " *When an assignment is too hard or too easy, students will be more likely to misbehave.*

Teachers should be aware of these four teaching practices and deliberately use them when working with students. We can't all be Mrs. Park, but we can learn how to effectively deal with our students.

Opening and Closing Class

The best-managed classes follow a routine for opening and closing class. The routine gives comfort and structure to children from chaotic homes and boosts their chances of success for the rest of the day.

1. Teacher greets students at the door for a quick personal greeting. A few personal words go far in building a trusting relationship that is the backbone of a well-managed class.

2. Students know what to do as soon as they enter. Typically they put away their things and start an independent activity. This has been practiced so once students enter, they are busy while the teacher completes personal greetings and deals with any urgent issues.

How Mrs. Park Did It

1 Relationships

2. Safety and Danger

3. Organization

4. Difficulty

3. After the greetings and students have had a chance to start the independent activity, the teacher briefly discusses the activity with the class before moving on to the teacher-led activities. You want to show that, as a teacher, you value their work and think it's important enough to spend some classroom time on it. Other routines are done at this time, lunch count, school announcements,

pledge of allegiance, and so forth.

4. You have the schedule of the day posted and briefly go over each item. You encourage curiosity and anticipation. Build some suspense as you tell them what they are going to learn and who they will be at the end of the day. When you do this, they are much more likely to learn it.

> *Time you spend practicing an efficient closing will result in a year-long gain of instructional time. A wall chart with directions can help during the first days of school.*

5. Clear up any questions/concerns before launching into the first lesson. If something upsetting happened on the playground prior to class, it needs to be addressed so students can focus.

6. Closing class and getting students ready to go home can result in a huge loss of instructional time if done poorly. Decide what you must accomplish during this time and practice it. For example, essential learnings reinforced, backpacks must be packed, chairs put up, trash and recycling dealt with and so forth. Time you spend practicing an efficient closing will result in a year-long gain of instructional time. A wall chart with directions can help during the first days of school.

Four Guidelines for Using Videos Effectively

It won't take long for a new teacher to find out how powerful a video is to get the attention of students. Because this tool is so effective at grabbing students' attention, you should be careful not to miss out on the power of a video to engage students and provide motivation.

1.   Before showing a video clip, be sure to give your students a task. For example, "I'm going to show you a 3-minute video clip on empathy and how it can help you make and keep friends. I want you to think about this as you

watch it, and imagine how you could use the ideas here at school."

If you just say, "Here's a video clip," then show it, your students miss out on a valuable learning opportunity.

> " *Avoid showing a whole video clip, when a short piece will serve your purpose. This is to avoid losing precious instructional time and diluting the emphasis on what you want your students to learn.*

2.   Avoid showing a whole video clip, when a short piece will serve your purpose. This is to avoid losing precious instructional time and diluting the emphasis on what you want your students to learn.

3.   Use a video clip as a reward if it's brief and supports serious instructional goals. For example, during a literature unit, if you are learning how film makers and authors connect the beginning of films to the end, show just the first and last 3 minutes of a Disney classic before studying how the author of your class novel follow the same connection rules. Tell your students to pay attention to TV shows and movies they watch at home to see how visual storytellers make these connections.

You don't want to be the teacher who shows a 90-minute video with a lame connection to academic goals. Using instructional time to show a whole movie, unless it is a strong, justifiable fit to your instructional goals, can be a loss of valuable instructional time and casts shade on all educators.

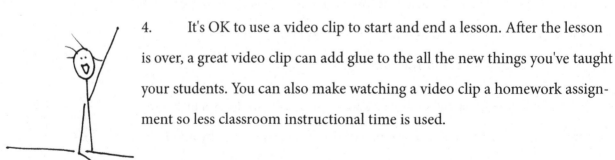

4.   It's OK to use a video clip to start and end a lesson. After the lesson is over, a great video clip can add glue to the all the new things you've taught your students. You can also make watching a video clip a homework assignment so less classroom instructional time is used.

Five Must-Do Activities for the First Week of School

1. Relationships

The relationships you build on the first week will make it much easier to work through behavior and academic problems later on. It's especially critical to start out well with your most difficult students whether it's the shy student who can't write to the behaviorally challenged, undiagnosed ADHD student.

One of the most effective methods to build relationships includes doing an **interest survey**. Once you know that your main behavior problem likes his hamster and Nike shoes, you can bring that up with him daily as a neutral and safe topic. Also, your students may have a profound expertise in popular music, transformers, or unicorns. You can use these as hooks to get them involved in lessons and view you as someone who really knows them. Students learn better when new knowledge is linked with topics they are familiar with, so it's a good idea to include popular culture in your lessons.

> *Using instructional time to show a whole movie, unless it is a strong, justifiable fit to your instructional goals, can be a loss of valuable instructional time and casts shade on all educators.*

If you know about an especially difficult student, call home on the first day to say something nice about that student and ask for suggestions to make the year go well. This will make future calls easier.

> *The teacher-student relationship is the most profound component of effective classroom management.*

Establish a habit of having something for your students to do when they first enter the class, so you can greet them by name each day.

> *Once you know that your main behavior problem likes his hamster and Nike shoes, you can bring that up with him every day as a neutral and safe topic.*

2. Routines

It turns out that teaching your students how to do everything from sharpening their pencil, to lining up for lunch, to transitioning from math to reading, will save hours and hours of instructional time though the school year. Sometimes it's helpful to ask a student or students to demonstrate a new routine before asking the class to do it.

Spend time to point out models and praise students who follow the routine. If you realize a routine is not quite right, change the name of it and re-teach it. For example, "Now it's the second week of school, and this is when we turn in our papers the Mountain Way. We put our papers in the top basket."

Highly stressed children, whether the source is from a Covid pandemic or other cause, find comfort in routine. When a powerful stressing event happens, like a death of a student or staff, falling back to routine is the way to go as well a spending some class time addressing student concerns.

3. Assessment/Observations

Teachers are assessing their students daily. It's pretty easy to find out who gets work done, who loses things and who can pay attention to stories. Use a class list or seating chart sheet to jot down notes and observations. This will come in handy during parent conferences and report-card time.

You don't need to do a technical, published assessment to get a general idea of how your students perform. For example, during Sustained Silent Reading

(SSR), you can ask each student to read to you for 2 minutes from a student-selected text. This should give you enough information to know what your students are capable of as a class to know where to go next. Be sure to take notes about these meetings.

4. Attention

You can teach your students not to pay attention. This is especially true of high ability and ELL students. If you don't grab the attention of your highest ability students right away, they will learn to tune you out since they will unconsciously decide they don't need you.

> *You don't need to do a technical, published assessment to get a general idea of how your students perform.*

Why mention ELL, English Language Learners, in the same breath as your gifted? Imagine if you were in a class where they only spoke Turkish. Soon you would not pay attention or expect to understand the teacher. Gifted and ELL students share the same problem: establishing a habit of not paying attention. Often these ELL students are quiet and compliant so they don't demand extra attention, but it's vital to get them engaged right off.

The best way to do this is to pair ELL students with a dual-language buddy, if available, or a nurturing student who is constantly checking for understanding. Consider changing these buddies occasionally to reduce impact on the rest of your class.

> *Highly stressed children, whether the source is from a pandemic or other cause, find comfort in routine.*

> *You can teach your students not to pay attention.*

5. Last Day of School Preparation

During the first week, you can set up a powerful and effective last day of school. Decide what activities on that last day would help your students feel proud of their progress and feel confident for the next year. Look back at the early interest inventory of what the student likes and dislikes. You can include questions on this about your students' concerns and hopes for the year. These are fun to look at the end of the year.

I tell the class it's a secret interest inventory, because it's not shared with other students. Do not imply that you won't share the information with parents or law enforcement, because you might become a liar if students reveal abuse or that they are in other danger.

If you can start out the year well, it will give you much more room to make mistakes and still be an effective teacher. If you can end the year well, you can feel confident in sending your students out into the future.

Working with Young Children

Nowhere in education is management and preparation more critical than early childhood education. Here's an example of an early childhood literacy period to show what I mean.

When teaching literacy skills to very young students, addressing a lesson directly to six students can be far more efficient than trying the same lesson with 24. When you can look them in the eye from three feet away, kids can more easily focus and absorb instruction.

> *If you can start out the year well, it will give you much more room to make mistakes and still be an effective teacher.*

When a lesson is this intimate, your ability to assess their progress is also improved. You know immediately if you need to change or adapt your instruction.

The "Graduation" Ceremony

If you students are moving from one grade to another, it can be an ego-strengthening activity to have a ceremony. Some elements to include in your ceremony:

‣ A touch. I use a Harry Potter-style magic wand. I touch the student and declare that she is now a fifth grader.

‣ A 30-second personalized speech about how proud you are of each student before touching him or her with the wand.

‣ A chorus response after each child is touched. All the students say the name of the person touched and something like, *"Eric, you will be a great fifth grader."*

‣ A piece of candy that they all pop in their mouths at the same time.

This presents a problem. If you are in a corner with 6 kindergartners, what are the other 18 doing? If you set them a task, and they don't do it, you really must stop instruction with your 6, and get the others back on track. If you don't, you are teaching them that they don't need to follow directions.

The best way to handle this situation is to have engaging independent activities available for the 18. I suggest you manage this with the use of learning stations. A station is an independent learning activity that a group of students can participate in for a set amount of time - usually 20 minutes. If you create 3 stations (the fourth station is you and your 6 students) and each day rotate students to a new one, you'll have a productive use of four, twenty minute small group lessons.

Be wary of overusing technology. How do you know if you are overusing it? Do a screen time assessment to see how many minutes of exposure your students are getting at school. The Mayo Clinic suggests a one-hour limit to high quality screen time for 5-year olds. Keep in mind that your kids are getting some or all of that at home. You don't want to be the person in your students' lives who is giving them too much.

A set of learning stations might look like this.

The first one might be a coloring station where kindergartners color and cut out math shapes based on a previous math lesson. The following day they move to a table to do a story-sequencing activity based on a literacy lesson, and in the next station, they are to take paper hearts and lace to make a valentine for their family. Of course, the fourth station is when they meet with you.

In a perfect world, this kindergarten class would have an instructional aide or parent volunteer to help students with their stations. Since this isn't always available, a "buddy" from a fifth grade class or even a more mature classmate might be a helper.

> *When a lesson is this intimate, your ability to assess their progress is also improved.*

Whatever your resources, students need to be trained in these two social skills:

1. Independence. When you are back with a group, they need to solve minor problems without disturbing the small instructional group that's meeting with you. If you don't do this, your whole instructional period

could be upended by a dried up glue stick.

2. Work behavior. They need to have fun and be productive without being loud. This means they must share and show kindness to their classmates as they keep their voices at a reasonable level.

When students learn these social skills, their academic and social progress begins to take great leaps forward. Students coming from highly stressed environments might take far longer to learn these skills.

If your class is mostly composed of under-resourced students, you may find that you'll spend the first six weeks of school just teaching them these "soft" skills, so you can later focus on academics. Check to see what other teachers at your grade level are doing; some may have found that teaching nearly everything whole-group works better for their population.

I'm suggesting to anyone teaching K-1 to work with a mentor or study the topic in depth.

When students learn the social skills, their academic and social progress begin to take great leaps forward. Students coming from highly stressed environments might take far longer to learn these skills.

Teaching Strategy

Using Post-its and a Continuum

Line as an Assessment Tool to Create Engagement

Imagine this, you have a long line going across a wall. On one side, a line says "Strongly Agree" on the other, "Strongly Disagree". This is a tool to help your students become engaged in a lesson and to serve as an assessment tool for you.

Let's say you are doing a unit on the Revolutionary War. Prior to instruction, pose a judgment statement like: The Revolutionary War was a good war. You give students a post-it. They put their name on it then on the back, they draw a copy of the continuum line and put a dot where they plan to put their post-it. You have them draw this line and put the dot so they won't just copy where their classmates put their post-its.

You tell them that after each lesson in the unit, they will be able to move their post-it one way or the other, but only if they can explain their reasoning.

With their name is up in front of everyone, students will be very interested in learning about the Revolutionary War period. At the end of each lesson, you can assign students to groups of 3 and they can discuss their thinking with each other prior to moving their post-it. You can roam during these discussions to get an idea of what your students have gained from the lesson, and where you need to take the next lesson.

Teacher Model Mrs. Anderson:

> *With their name is up in front of everyone, students will be very interested in learning about the Revolutionary War period.*

Maximizing the Benefits of a Class Discussion

Teachers recognize the value of a class discussion. Students can see peers excited about the curriculum and that infectious excitement translates to interest and motivation.

One of the problems with class discussion is that some students avoid becoming engaged and give little thought to the topic. I observed how Mrs. Anderson, an energetic upper grade teacher, figured out how to pull everyone into her discussions.

First, Mrs. Anderson told the students that she was going to pass out a skinny, yellow paper. She instructed the students to put their name on the paper, read it over silently and think about their answer to the first question, but not to write anything besides their name. Then she confirmed her directions were understood before passing out the paper. The shape and color of the paper added novelty to the lesson.

It was obvious that students had been trained in how to efficiently distribute papers. In moments, the papers were passed out. Mrs. Anderson was free to roam and point out models: students who were following directions. By identifying models, Mrs. Anderson was able to capture the attention of all her students.

After students had a few minutes to examine the first question, Mrs. Anderson explained how she expected the students' answers to look. She put up a model answer on the screen, and asked students to raise their hand if they had any questions.

Mrs. Anderson then announced that students would have 3 minutes to record a rough-draft answer on their sheet. Afterwards they would share their sheet with a partner assigned by Mrs. Anderson.

By giving them a time limit, Mrs. Anderson let her students know that they had no time to waste and needed to get started. When she informed them they would share their answers with a partner, she plugged into the students' desires to look good in front of their peers.

Mrs. Anderson told her students to begin and snapped her fingers. The snap seemed to wake up a quiet boy in the back who immediately began to work on his sheet. Nearly 100% of students were complying.

Mrs. Anderson approached Elle, a shy girl who appeared very uncomfortable. Later, Mrs. Anderson explained to me that since Elle was new and far behind the other students, Mrs. Anderson told the new girl just to copy the model from the board. Presto! 100% on-task students.

After students had finished their partner sharing—where they were encouraged to change and/or develop their answers based on their peer interactions—Mrs. Anderson asked if any students wanted to share their answers with the class. A forest of hands went up and an amazing class discussion ensued.

Mrs. Anderson put the key points on a virtual poster as students shared. She then asked students to think about the list and name the five most important items on the list. She had students do this independently, then with a partner. This injected fresh energy into the discussion and motivated students into building connections between items on the list.

What amazed me was how she was able to engage every student in the discussion. She said the worksheet caused all students to think about the topic intensely prior to the discussion, so they could all contribute. Her students were engaged in partner discussions where they had to give evidence to support their views. Her classroom routines allowed her to move efficiently through her lesson. Having students pick out the most important items on the list caused her students to think deeply about each item. The chart would be used to introduce the next lesson.

> *What amazed me was how she was able to engage every student in the discussion.*

Reader's Quiz!

Read the Model Teacher: Mrs. Anderson Article. Which of these can you find?

➤ Raising level of concern

➤ Lowering level of concern

➤ Start signal

➤ Use of practiced routines

➤ Use of novelty

➤ Models/examples

➤ Use of compare/contrast

➤ Total class engagement

➤ Discussion preparation

➤ Avoiding dead time

➤ Checking for understanding

➤ Making socially insecure students feel safe

➤ Using discussion to add interest and energy to her lesson

➤ Teacher roaming during independent time

➤ Helping students build connections with new and old knowledge

➤ _____

Why Not More Early-Childhood Strategies?

When I was planning this book, I wanted to have a comprehensive section on what I had learned when I worked with my first graders and other young students. What hit me as I was writing is that this group is a world onto itself.

To do the subject justice, would dominate the whole book. So I'm suggesting to anyone teaching K-1 to work with a mentor or study the topic in depth. Many of the techniques in this book work well with young children, but some don't. For example, kindergartners generally are not too concerned with their peer's opinions, but tend to be very much concerned with what their teacher's stuffed animal or puppet thinks.

9
Certain Kids

Typically, your special students are outliers who are actually the most fragile and sometimes the hardest kids to love. It's OK if you don't love all your students, but you must form a bond with them in order to be the most effective teacher you can be.

As I say in Chapter 12, it's possible to be a highly skilled classroom manager and still have students who are unable to be managed.

Keep in mind, no matter how skilled you are, you could end up with a student or students who are so outside the norm, that you'll feel like a failure. If you find yourself in such circumstances, you need to seek help from administrators, colleagues and counselors. You need to be kind to yourself in order to get through the year intact.

Case Study: The Attention Deficit/Impulsive Student

Steven always showed remorse when he caused a problem. And he caused a lot of problems. That first day of school he looked up at me, pale eyes full of self-doubt, and asked me if he did OK on his first paper. He hadn't. Steven wasn't timid or stupid, he just expected to disappoint the people he loved. Steven was diagnosed with an attention disorder.

Despite Steven's heart of gold, he could not control his attention problems or hyperactivity. As a result, he entered my fifth grade class fully expecting to be a "bad boy," yet yearning to please.

After the first day, I realized I had made more behavior corrections for Steven than all other students combined. By the end of the first week, he probably had many times the behavior corrections of all my other students. This wasn't sustainable, either for Steven or for me.

Talking with other teachers and reading up on the subject, I came up with five strategies to make sure Steven and I had a great year.

What worked for Steven and Me — 5:1

My goal became to give Steven five positive affirmations for every correction he received. This strategy would become the most important and effective of anything Steven and I did to make his fifth grade year a good one.

Since Steven was nearly powerless to control his impulsivity, I had to become creative to make sure he was constantly successful in other areas and try to figure out ways to lower the number of behavior corrections. I also spent a great deal of time watching Steven to catch him "being good". It's a powerful thing when a teacher is looking for

"

Put yourself in Steven's place for a moment. How would you feel if, in the course of a day, your supervisor told you dozens of times that you were making mistakes, being rude or not paying attention?

positive instead of negative behaviors in a student.

Put yourself in Steven's place for a moment. How would you feel if, in the course of a day, your supervisor told you dozens of times that you were making mistakes, being rude or not paying attention? It would wear on you, right? Some teachers might be crushed with just one critical comment from a supervisor. What could I do to make sure Steven received lots of affirmations?

As often as Steven would interrupt someone, it would have been easy to think he didn't care about others' feelings. In fact, the opposite was true. When I made him the "super buddy" of Greg, the special needs student, who came in for certain activities, Steven showed a degree of empathy and tenderness that brought confidence to both himself and Greg. I could use time-helping-in-Greg's-class as a reward for Steven.

I also put Steven in charge of our classroom fish tank. I trained him in the secret arts of tank maintenance and fish care. He became the fish boss, rising in social rank among his less-knowledgeable peers. Keeping the feeding and maintenance schedule might have also made Steven more aware of dates and times. Like many ADHD sufferers, Steven was horribly disorganized. Also, fish bosses must be out of their seat to check on the fish, so I didn't need to tell him to go back to his seat so often.

Steven and I came up with codes that signaled he was doing well or if he needed to knock it off. If I touched his paper, book or desk, it meant that I liked what I was seeing. If I shook my head at him, he knew to stop or pause doing something. If I needed a student to model something, I tried

> *Since Steven was nearly powerless to control his impulsivity, I had to become creative to make sure he was constantly successful in other areas and try to figure out ways to lower the number of behavior corrections.*

to use Steven as a demonstrator or helper. This got him out of his seat and often out of trouble.

Finding out that he was a valued member of the class gave Steven a new confidence. His classmates saw him as the lovable clown he had been in previous grades, but also as a successful and respected class member. With his classmates providing some of the positive encounters for Steven, it boosted him even more.

Steven and I had our good days and bad. Sometimes, he seemed to need 10 positives for every correction, and other times, he got along great with the 5:1 ratio or fewer. Overall, he and I developed a close working relationship built on trust and respect based on the 5:1 plan.

The "Bad" Boy

Jeremy was "bad". He stole a pencil box from Margaret, broke it, refused to apologize and denied everything despite being caught in the act. Furthermore, he started cussing at me when I confronted him with the evidence.

After I realized that I wasn't getting anywhere with him, I called home. His dad answered. I told Jeremy's father what happened and asked him to have a talk with his angry son.

The following day, Jeremy came to school with facial bruising. He told me he fell off his bike then started crying. I think his dad hit him.

Now who's bad? His dad? Or is it I? After calling Child Services to report suspected abuse, they said they would put Jeremy on their watch list, but there was not enough information to pursue the matter any farther.

A week later, Jeremy stole and broke something from another student's desk. It was my second year of teaching, and I didn't know what to do. I didn't want to be the bad guy.

If I called home, Jeremy might get beaten. If I didn't, his parents would not be aware of problems Jeremy was having at school.

I discussed it with Jeremy. Without admitting his father abused him, he asked if I could call his mom at her work instead. When I got his mother on the phone I explained to her that Jeremy was punished at a school and didn't need any further disciplining. I don't like the work, *punish*, but I felt I had to be very clear to Jeremy's parents.

What her son needed, I suggested, was a chance to say his piece at home and then receive advice for future situations. He needs to know that their family doesn't approve of stealing, but that they love their son – not his actions.

> " *If you wear jeans and sweatshirts, you are not modeling professional behavior, and leaving your students without a clear image of professional appearance.*

It was a tough year for Jeremy. His fragile family eventually broke up, and he moved away. However, I learned that whenever I called a parent to report misbehavior, I would begin the call with an explanation that the child had already been punished, so the parents didn't need to further punish. I told them they were free to offer guidance to their wayward child. It's not a perfect solution, but it's not bad. Jeremy was held accountable for his poor choices at school, parents were notified and given a chance to demonstrate their love and support for their son.

> *Many educators feel uncomfortable with the word "punish". The much preferred word is consequence. I use the first word with parents because it's nearly unambiguous.*

Many educators feel uncomfortable with the word *punish*. The much preferred word is *consequence*. I use the first word with parents because it's nearly unambiguous. The child needs no further punishment.

Ten Assets You Can Provide Economically Deprived Children

There has been extensive work done on how to teach children from economically deprived homes, but this is just a quick sketch. This subject is extensive and worth exploring on your own with literature that specializes in studies of the special needs of this population. View this part as just dipping your toe into the deep waters of dealing with under resourced kids.

❯ Build and Maintain Positive Relationships

> *I learned that whenever I called a parent to report misbehavior, I would begin the call with an explanation that the child had already been punished, so the parents didn't need to further punish.*

This is probably your most important strategy for success with these kids. Show interest in your students, their activities, family, friends and hobbies. Ask questions and refer back to

their answers in future conversations. Use the information you gathered during the interest survey you gave at the year's beginning and bring up music, films, and other cultural references during lessons that show you care and believe in their ability to succeed.

❯ Model Mainstream Dress and Language

Some students from poverty have few models of success. They need to see how to dress and speak to be part of the culture of economic power. Do not try to fit in with their culture even if you are from it. They need to learn how to dress and speak in a way that will allow them to enter into the economic mainstream if they so choose. You don't want to make them feel bad over the way they dress and speak since their culture is every bit as important and genuine as yours. You **do** want to model and praise conventional speech. You can even call it a different language - the language of power. If you wear jeans and sweatshirts, you are not modeling professional behavior, and leaving your students without a clear image of professional appearance. Dress professionally.

❯ Model Healthy Emotional Responses To Daily Life

Many of these students have little experience with an emotionally healthy adult. Show them

> **You Can Use Literature to Teach Emotional and Social Skills:**
> Literature: stories, biographies, plays and so forth, are a great way to have class discussions about characters' emotional and social skills like kindness, gratitude, perseverance, acceptance, empathy and so forth.

healthy emotional responses to frustrations, successes, tragedy and so forth. Show them how to express hope, kindness, empathy, humor, joy and other positive emotions.

‣ Model Professional Demeanor

Imagine you are at the dentist's office and your dentist yells and cries when you haven't flossed as she suggested. You wouldn't expect that and likely find it disorienting. Let your students see a calm, confident adult. Avoid showing anger, crying, yelling or otherwise acting less than professional. Forgive yourself when you make a mistake and resolve to do better. This can be hard to do.

> *Let your students see a calm, confident adult. Avoid getting mad, crying, yelling or otherwise acting less than professional.*

‣ Make Sure Your Students Experience Academic Success

As a high school student, I once had a teacher who said that anyone who didn't want to learn could sit on the bench in the back of the class. One boy did. Don't tolerate failure lightly. For one thing, children are too young to consent to ignorance and failure. Make the learning of academic skills your priority. Kids from poor backgrounds often don't recognize their accomplishments, so you have to point it out to them and tell them how to feel about it.

‣ Create a Safe Classroom

Picture a bucket of crabs all yearning to get out of the bucket and into the water. One reaches up to the lip of the bucket, and the others pull it back down. Sometimes students feel uncomfortable with success and will pull down your high fliers with teasing or mocking. Make sure that students feel comfortable taking academic risks and feel proud of themselves and their classmates.

Teach your students to celebrate and strive for success.

> **Help Students Develop a Sense of Control**

Students from poverty or other stressors often feel a profound lack of control and do not understand that their choices can influence their life. Make it clear to students that they have the ability to make behavioral choices that will affect them. Point out how students' choices are influencing their lives. When a student does

---

Ten Assets You Can Provide Economically Deprived Children

1. Positive relationships

2, Modeled mainstream dress and language

3 Modeled healthy emotional responses

4. Modeled professional demeanor

5. Academic success

6. A safe classroom

7. A sense of control

8. Knowledge of acceptable behaviors

9. A teacher who reaches out to withdrawn students

10. Techniques for calming themselves

something well or badly, use the idea of **choice** in your comments. "I'm sorry you chose not to do this assignment."

➤ Teach acceptable alternative behaviors to inappropriate responses.

Probably the most effective way to do this is through role play. Your students practice appropriate responses enough so it becomes their first response. Another way to teach this is to have your students imagine themselves acting appropriately and to explain what they could have chosen to do after they make a mistake.

➤ Reach out to quiet and withdrawn students.

It's easy to bring your mind to focus on your active, loud rule-testers. These highly-stressed students demand your attention. Some students react to stress in other ways. They have special needs, too, even if they are quiet. In my experience, this is especially true, but not limited, to girls.

➤ Teach students how to calm themselves.

If you can trust the upset student out of your vision, it's generally easier for students to calm down when they are away from whatever or whomever set them off. As I said earlier, I like to set them a task of getting a drink down the hall and returning to class.

However, you need to teach them how to use this away time. If, with each step they take away from your classroom, they count up all the ways they've been harmed, they will just feed and build anger into fury.

Train them to imagine they are becoming calmer with each step they take, so that by the time they return to class, they are calm and ready to learn. I like to do this by telling them that's how they'll feel, and challenge the student to notice how each step takes away bad feelings and adds calm.

This training works best when the student is calm or after breathing exercises, meditation, progressive relaxation or just a jog around the playground.

The Importance of Teaching Vocabulary and Background Knowledge

The Himba language, spoken in Namibia, has only one word for the colors blue and green: zuzu. Some researchers, notably Jules Davidoff of University of London, claimed that tribal members could not distinguish between color swatches of blue and green. If they have no word for it, they can't see it.

> *If children are not exposed to an idea, they may be unable to perceive it on their own.*

When older deaf people were first taught the American Sign Language, there existed no word for *simultaneous*. As a result, this group of people consistently failed a graphic test that any typical first grader would pass. The test results were so startling, that several researchers wanted to rerun all these assessments. In the interim, many of the subjects had been exposed to a younger deaf population, who had acquired the word for *simultaneous*. Those subjects passed the test.

What does this have to do with teaching?

It might mean that if children are not exposed to an idea, they may be unable to perceive it on their own. If ideas like *blue* and *simultaneous* do not exist for people who have never been taught them, then what does it mean when researchers claim that under-resourced children enter school having heard tens of millions fewer words than their wealthier peers?

> *Nearly always after performing a math experiment, reading a piece of literature, or examining a historical document, I'll think of my gifted eighth graders and my first question will be, "What did you notice?"*

Especially if you teach in a high-poverty area, you need to spend part of every lesson teaching vocabulary and the background concepts behind the words. Some researchers claim that a student needs to learn 88,000 words between grades 3 and 9.

Here are three ways you can help your students develop their vocabulary.

1. Stop your instruction to check understanding whenever you think a word or concept might be unknown to your students. You can provide a super fast mini-lesson on the word, then return to instruction. Think of this like a commercial during a Super Bowl game. If not overdone, it won't ruin the lesson, and may be easy for your students to remember since the new word has important connections. Keep these new words on a Word Wall to review.

2. Encourage your students to collect words from their reading. You can provide your students a small blank book and encourage your students to collect verbs, proper nouns, modifying words and so forth.

3. Provide times for students to interact with their new words. For example, have them group words by meaning or other criteria.

Meeting the Needs of Gifted Students

After living in Europe for several years and spending far too much time prowling art museums, photographing artwork and studying it, I felt confident about teaching a unit on Renaissance Painting to my class of gifted eighth graders. Our unit was to be culminated by a field trip to the Renaissance section of the local art museum.

Our guide couldn't make it, so the museum curator filled in. Near the end of the tour, the curator gestured to the stunning collection of Renaissance religious art and asked if there were any questions.

Chris, a handsome red headed boy asked, "*Why doesn't the figure of Mary ever actually touch the Christ child?*"

The question blew my mind. I had never noticed this detail. Then Beth asked, "*Why does Mary always wear a rose colored blouse?*" Another mind-blowing observation. The questions kept coming and the curator loved it. She led us into an exciting and deep conversation about the symbolic conventions of the painters and the religious thinking of the era.

> *No matter how skilled a manager you are, it's possible to have a student or students who are so outside the norm, that you'll feel like a failure.*

This is where I decided that one of the ways gifted students are different from us normal people, is that they notice more.

It might be easy to say that all students are gifted in their own way, but when you really meet one, it's very clear that this student is special.

Intellectual assessment tests don't always identify gifted children, so teachers need to use common sense to see that some learners are gifted even if not identified by a test. I suggest you not limit special assignments just to identified intellectually gifted students, but open these special assignments to any willing student. An average student, who's gifted with extreme motivation, could also find great benefits from doing a special assignment.

I have five rules I apply to my classroom with the needs of gifted students in mind:

Rule 1: Never tell a student something he/she already knows.

This means you teach by attempting to draw out the information from your students. Let's say you are doing a lesson on emotions for a first grade class. You are pretty sure the students know *mad, sad, glad.* But you want them to expand their knowledge to emotions like *frustration, excitement, and anxiety.*

Meeting the Needs of Gifted Students

➤ Never tell them what they already know.

➤ Offer engaging assignment extensions and excuse them from unnecessary practice.

➤ Construct open-ended assignments.

➤ Group gifted students together from time to time.

➤ Avoid putting them in a corner with an advanced workbook.

Before you tell them any of these words, see if you can get a student to name them. Often gifted children feel frustrated when they are stuck in a class where they are being taught what they already know. Interestingly, these students often find the class fascinating if they are the source of the knowledge.

After performing a math experiment, reading a piece of literature, or examining a historical document, I'll think of my gifted eighth graders and my first question will be, *"What did you notice?"* If students are not used to this type of question, you will need to use **wait time** to teach them how to respond to this question.

Since you never tell a gifted student something they already know, then when you find something new for that child, make sure they recognize they are learning something new. Have them tell their parents what they learned that day, so their parents know you are challenging their child.

I've said things like this to my students, *"So no one has their hands up. Not one student in this class knows the next number in this sequence."* You look at your gifted student, *"This is what you will tell your parents you learned today."* Then I explain how to find the next number. I make sure my gifted students learn something new each day, and are prepared to explain it to their parents.

Rule 2: Offer assignment extensions for ambitions students or students who finish quickly.

For example, in a fourth grade class we were reading a book by Beverly Cleary. Prior to starting the Cleary unit, I displayed a Beverly Cleary Award. Every child who completed the book (and I made sure we all did) would get this award. However, if a student read another book by the author, a foil star would be attached for each novel beyond the class-read book. Gifted, and many other students really worked hard for those stars. Also, gifted students need far less repetition to learn, so excuse them from doing the practice if you see they don't need it. This gives them time to try an extension.

Rule 3: Construct assignments with open-ended outcomes.

For example, if you give a gifted student something that's complete

when a blank is filled in, you are going to have a frustrated student. Instead, ask for thoughts, comparisons, summaries, and observations. If your gifted student turns in something banal, you can ask for more and really challenge that student.

Construct assignments that result in a project. If the outcome is project-oriented, your gifted student will learn more than you probably planned. During the Beverly Cleary unit, students had to write a chapter beginning that had all the elements of a Cleary chapter beginning.

The results were stunning, both gifted and stealth-gifted students surpassed my expectations. Offer assignment extensions that are open to all students, but you can assign these to your gifted students and remove any unnecessary assignments.

Rule 4: Group gifted students together from time to time.

Despite the fact that most of my groups are made up by drawing popsicle sticks (random), I make sure to put gifted students together for some projects. My reasoning is that these academic wonders so often find themselves in a place where they have to teach their less capable partners, instead of being taught themselves. Putting them with someone who can keep up or surpass them results in happy, thriving students.

Oppositional Defiant Disorder - *ODD*

This is a medical/behavioral disease that requires a medical diagnosis. You can't do that. Don't ever tell anybody that someone has this disease unless you are medically licensed. Just because a student has behavioral issues, doesn't mean they have ODD. ODD presents on a spectrum from something you can do your part to manage to something far beyond anything a teacher can do. Later in this section you'll see information about students showing some of the symptoms of ODD.

Rule 5: Avoid putting your gifted student alone in a corner with an advanced workbook.

You can accelerate students without isolating them. I suggest you keep the class together for the instruction part of the lesson, allowing the advanced students and other students to share what they know. During the independent part of the lesson, you have separate assignments for your high-fliers and struggling students. You also want to avoid giving just "more work" to advanced students, but instead, give work that takes into account what they already know.

If you follow these five rules, it turns out your other students will also respond well. You'll have a class where high cognitive functioning is encouraged and nurtured.

An Oppositional Student

Sometimes a student acts out to such a degree, that it interferes with their academic and social lives—as well as the learning of the rest of your class. These children are sometimes referred to as acting oppositional — or just oppositional.

> " *The only way I know of to overcome the problems associated with these students is to discipline yourself. You need to do the extra work to plan a strategy for helping your Emmas find success and make a good try at not limiting the rest of the class.*

Some mental health professionals warn that the withdrawn, quiet student might be more of a concern. That child might be suffering from depression, anxiety and possibly self harm behavior. Keep these kids on your radar even as you deal with oppositional students.

How might this look? Let's say after the science experiment, you gave the signal for clean up. But you notice Emma isn't cleaning up. Maybe she doesn't understand the signal. Maybe she loves repeating the experiment. Maybe she's just acting oppositional and always tests your rules.

You decide to identify a model to help Emma understand what you expect her to do, and point to a student in his proximity and say, *"Hey, I like the way Violet is cleaning up."*

> *Oppositional students can make your life uncomfortable, and cause you to avoid lessons that involve elements like wet paint, hot glue, rubber bands and so forth.*

Emma doesn't clean up, but now you know she understands what you expect.

You announce, *"Say, this clean up is going great. We'll be able to do another science experiment soon, since I can trust you to put things away so quickly."* Emma doesn't clean up, but now you know it isn't love of science that's causing her to ignore your rule.

You lower your voice so others can't hear you and talk to Emma, *"Hey, Emma. Looks like you enjoyed this science lesson. What are you supposed to do now?"* You always ask a question to redirect a student instead of repeating directions. This puts the onus on the student to formulate the reply and can take her mind off being oppositional. By keeping the behavior correction just between you and Emma, you remove her need to publicly resist your correction and allow her to save face.

Emma answers, *"I don't know what to do. You never told me."* The wrong reply on your part would be to remind her that you told her about clean up before the lesson started and you posted a list on

> *You always ask a question to redirect a student instead of repeating directions.*

the board. She'll just deny you said anything and try to get you into an argument. Don't get into an argument!

Instead, hide your frustration behind a mask of benign indifference and say something like, *"Maybe that's true, but you need to figure out what to do, and soon. I'd hate to have you late for lunch."* Then you turn away and pretend to ignore her while praising a diligent student who's complying with your clean up procedure.

When you said, *"late for lunch"* you hinted at the consequence she's facing if she doesn't start the clean up. By turning away from Emma, you've given her space to start the clean up without losing face. Showing obedience won't embarrass her.

> *Ask the counselor, special education teacher, your administrator or other interested party to observe in your class in order to get feedback/suggestions.*

It's at this point that you make a mental note to touch bases with Emma before the next science lesson asking her what she plans to do when it's clean up time. You can offer to have her start her clean up prior to other students if she needs more time to put her things away. This is a consequence she'll want to avoid, and it will raise the chances that she'll comply with the clean up procedure next time.

If she still resists clean up, you should act surprised so as not to reinforce her self-constructed role as someone who doesn't follow rules. You want her to think you expect her to go along with procedures.

Oppositional students can make your life uncomfortable, and cause you to avoid lessons that involve elements like wet paint, hot glue, rubber bands and so forth. It's not fair to the rest of your class. By meeting her ahead of the lesson, you can ask her if she's capable of dealing with rubber bands in a safe manner, and tell her you have an alternate assignment for students who can't handle dangerous items.

Where to Get Help

Student's family
Former teachers
Current teachers
Administration
Counselor/School Psychologist
Special Education Personnel
Attorney - district or union
Student's pediatrician (with parental approval)

The only way I know of to overcome the problems associated with these students is to discipline yourself. You need to do the extra work to plan a strategy for helping your Emmas find success and make a good try at not limiting the rest of the class. Elements of these strategies include giving Emma a role to play. [*"Now Emma, I know you want to learn."*], avoiding arguments, preparing her ahead of the lessons to follow directions, and having a set of soft-to-harsh consequences ready. I understand that this is really hard for nearly all teachers.

It's also a good idea to contact her parents when she's been behaving - so you don't need to deliver bad news with every parental contact. Ask her parents for advice. This might yield important information about Emma's life, let her parents know she's having problems, and show that you care about their daughter. Be sure to mention that they don't need to punish her for her past behavior so they don't take counter-productive harshly punitive actions. After contacting Emma's parents, keep notes on the contact and have a colleague sign and date the notes. (*See Notes on page 164.*)

If Emma has another teacher with whom she has fewer problems, ask to observe in that class to get ideas on how to better deal with her. Or have that teacher observe your interactions with Emma and give you feedback. Also, if possible, contact Em-

Three Ways to Help Your Oppositional Student

1. Show empathy: *"I can understand how that would make you angry, but you can't break things."*

2. Look for and point out progress: *"Look how long it's been since your last meltdown. You are getting things under control. You should feel good about that."*

3. Provide a cool down strategy to use before the pot boils over: *"You look upset take this paper to the office. You'll feel calmer with each step after the walk."*

ma's former teachers for advice.

It's possible that you will never be able to get Emma to a place where she can participate with the rest of the class. It's at this point that you should start a behavior log for her.

At a quiet time, you can write log or record a voice memo documenting Emma's behavior. Always include date, time and who else could corroborate your log. Be sure to avoid any language that sound judgmental or prejudiced, but stick to the facts. Judgmental language could be taken as bias and weaken your log.

Ask the counselor, special education teacher, your administrator or other interested party to observe in your class in order to get feedback/suggestions. Keep a log of what they tell you. Later, if Emma gets herself in real trouble, you'll have information that can help the school gather resources for Emma and protect you against any lawsuits.

It might be possible that Emma is so problem-plagued, that she can't ever fit in with a typical class. This is not a decision that a general education teacher can make alone. If you keep a good log you can contact the special education department to get information about an evaluation.

Prior to this, show the log to your administrator and ask for advice. By showing the log to the administrator and asking for advice, you are not a teacher complaining about a difficult student, but a responsible teacher who keeps the administration informed.

Add any administrative advice to your log and how it worked out. No matter how well-managed your class, it's possible you can't reach certain children thus requiring additional professional resources and interventions.

Case Study: The Unengaged Student

Chris didn't care. He appeared to be easy-going and relaxed academically but also socially. His easy smile made him likable enough, but his lackadaisical approach to learning really made him stand out. Typically, I would find him daydreaming as he stared out the window, and he seemed utterly comfortable with uncompleted work.

> *My plan with Chris was to put gentle, persistent pressure on him to complete work, then motivate him to desire the feelings of satisfaction over his accomplishments.*

If I asked him to get started on his assignment, he would do that, but seemed entirely dependent on my attention to continue working. As it wasn't really practical for me to stand behind him during every independent work period, I had to find a way to help him become productive. My middle school colleagues assured me that "work completion" was the key to middle school success even over cognitive ability.

I realized I had to help him learn to desire work completion. He would enter middle school the following year and have four to six different teachers. They might not prioritize a quiet, smiley student who seemed content to sit in the back and under-perform. My plan with Chris was to put gentle, persistent pressure on him to complete work, then motivate him to desire the feelings of satisfaction over his accomplishments. With the help of parental support, he and I started his journey.

This actually worked. At first I saw no changes. For six weeks he resolutely stuck to his lax work-completion habits. But by the end of the fourth quarter, he was his same relaxed self, but needed no extraordinary pushing to complete his work. He just did his work and turned it in. He went off to middle school, and I never saw him again until 20 years later when he called me up and asked to meet for coffee.

He told me he had a successful career in the military and felt he owed it all to me. Whenever a student credits me for their success, I turn it around and tell them that I was just their cheering section. They need to give themselves all the credit and gain the self-confidence.

I'm sure Chris had lots of wonderful teachers and mentors on his journey, but it made me happy that he learned the soft skill of work completion with me.

Making Effective Contemporaneous Notes

If you think you might need these notes for a legal matter, consult an attorney. I'm not an attorney, so this is my layman's advice.

> Factual – write nothing you would be uncomfortable to read out in a meeting.

> Made in ink at the time of an event or as soon after as is practical.

> Dated - have colleague initial the date on the day you make the entry.

> Original and not copied from elsewhere.

> No erasures - draw a thin line over errors.

> No leaves or pages to be torn out.

> No blank spaces - mark over blank spaces with lines.

> No writing between lines.

> No separate pieces of paper.

> Amendments to be initialed.

> Store in secure place.

10
Families

You can't fix a broken or dysfunctional family. Here's what you can do.

Part of the fun of being a teacher is establishing relationships with students and their families. The family relationships can last for many years and let you see what happens to your students long after they leave your care.

Picture educating a child as a three-legged stool. It stands stable and effective with the three legs: teacher-student-family. You'll make the most progress with your students if you can enlist and engage their families in the process. As you read through this chapter, think about how you can adapt and enhance any suggestions to fit your teaching situation.

Calling Parents

If you don't attempt to involve parents in your instruction, you are making your job a lot harder. This chapter has ideas on how to get parents to help you educate their child. As you read this, think of other ways you can connect with your families.

You might be amazed by the effectiveness of an early "Sunshine" call to parents during the first two weeks of school. Your call should be positive and express hope for a great year for their child. Be sure to say something specific about their child to show parents you really know something about their kid. You want to avoid email when contacting parents about important, specific comments about their child. Misinterpreted emails can result in an enormous waste of time. It's actually more efficient to call.

The Sunshine Call is a good time to ask if parents have any concerns about their child's year. Make notes about these, and touch bases with parents on the topic and bring it up during conferences.

> *I always make the first calls to the parents of the students most likely to misbehave before they will get one of the "bad calls" from me.*

I always make the first calls to the parents of the students most likely to misbehave before they will get one of the "bad calls" from me. Usually there's a honeymoon period during the first week of school, where students with behavior problems tend to avoid trouble. If possible, you want to make sure you call before Johnny gets in trouble.

You can honestly tell Johnny's parents that he seems to have gotten a handle on his oppositional behavior this year, and this could be his best year ever — if you call before Johnny gets in trouble. Then you can act surprised and concerned when Johnny acts up later.

His family will be more likely to view you as an ally.

You can also pull Johnny aside and tell him you are going to call his parents to tell them what a great start he's having this year. This can help Johnny and his family to rebuild their views of Johnny's relationship to school.

If you can get parents to see that you truly care about their child, a later call to explain a problem might go down better.

Faking it - Acting Confident When You Don't Feel It

Imagine going to the hospital for a medical procedure and a nurse tells you how bad the other nurses are. Then the doctor walks in and complains about her equipment and the building. How would you feel?

One huge mistake you can make is to whine and complain to parents, students and fellow teachers about your school, your class, and/or your co-workers. Also, if a parent prompts you to agree with a negative assessment of a staff member, it won't be long before the entire neighborhood knows your views. Soon your colleagues will not trust you. Not only does this reflect badly on you by projecting weak professional ethics, it can drain all the goodwill and enthusiasm from your support network.

> *Even if you feel utterly defeated by very real problems, I suggest that you fake a positive outlook for the year when talking to parents.*

Complaining can create a self-fulfilling prophecy where you expect things to go bad, and so they do.

This is not to say you don't advocate for your

students and yourself. You advocate in an upright, professional manner. You can be a strong supporter for your school and your students and still maintain a sterling professional comportment.

Even if you feel utterly defeated by very real problems, I suggest that you fake a positive outlook for the year when talking to parents. Tell students and parents that you are going to work hard to make this the best year ever for the children, and here's how they can help make sure that happens. More often than not, I've seen such a forced prophecy come true.

> *One huge mistake you can make is to complain to parents, students and fellow teachers about your school, your class, and your co-workers.*

If you profess a positive prediction for their children, you can still explain some of the hurdles that must be overcome, but never give parents an image of a teacher who's given up.

When it comes to problems at school, better than complaining to colleagues is to ask administrators and colleagues for advice on how to deal with situations that you find troublesome.

I would also suggest that you avoid hanging out with negative staff members if possible. They will bring you down and cast darkness where you need light. This might mean you need to avoid the staff room.

You also need to care for yourself by finding someone, hopefully outside of the school, with whom to vent your concerns. Do other things to help maintain your mental health: exercise, eat well and get enough sleep, and keep up with vaccines if you are able.

> *You also need to care for yourself by finding someone, hopefully outside of the school, with whom to vent your concerns.*

Forgive yourself when you make a mistake, and promise to do better. You owe it to yourself and your students to take good care of yourself.

Attempts to Censor

One year there were two third grade classes in my school, Mrs. Patel and mine. We shared a class set of *Charlotte's Web*. I used it first with my class as a classroom novel and sent the set over to Patel's classroom.

When Mrs. Patel, an experienced teacher, started the book, she nearly instantly had a visit from the principal. He informed her that two parents demanded she pick another book since *Charlotte's Web* had talking animals, and that kind of sorcery was against their religion.

Mrs. Patel tried to convince the principal that there was nothing wrong with the book, but the parents won. The class had to skip the novel unit, as a replacement set of books could not be acquired in time.

We should not let parents or political groups censor us, but we also need to remember that we need to serve the community and diligently seek to avoid predicable conflicts. It's a balancing act.

> "We educators should not impose our religious beliefs on our students, nor should parents censor or force educators to modify reasonable school-wide traditions or curricula.

We educators should not impose our religious or political beliefs on our students, nor should parents censor or force educators to modify reasonable school-wide traditions or curricula. If you think you may face strong parental concerns about what you're teaching, stay close to the state and local curriculum guidelines so you can hold up your hands and claim you are just doing your job if faced with complains.

At the risk of sounding inconsistent, it's a good idea to avoid using any religious symbols in your lessons unless they can be strongly connected to your curriculum.

We all learned a lesson from Mrs. Patel's experience. From then on, we sent home a list of books and units we were presenting to our classes and gave parents a chance to pull their children from the class. Better to have one student miss out than the whole class censored. Excused students could sit in the library and work on a packet.

A parent could still demand that we pull a book, but none ever did. Only once did a parent pull her child from a unit to sit in the library — and that was a human growth and development unit.

Kids hate to be pulled, and if you give parents a way to protect their child from *"bad things the school is doing"*, then you are very unlikely to be censored.

Later that same year, during a social studies unit on slavery, I wanted students to know how slaves communicated anti-slavery messages through slave songs. Many of these songs mentioned Mary or Jesus. My goal was not to send religious messages to my students, but to

> *Whenever I started a unit that could conceivably cause concern in any minority group, I offered a chance to opt out rather than get censored.*

> "It is the right of people to not listen to, and not read, anything they find offensive. But this right is limited: it does not give them the right to limit what others choose to hear or read.
>
> The only exception to this statement is with one's own children. Parents do have both a right, and an obligation, to react to what their children are listening to and reading.
>
> But that right and obligation is limited to their own children—not mine!"
>
> - Dr. David C. Berliner

help them learn and understand my social studies goals.

I sent a note home to parents explaining the songs, and why we were singing them. Any parent who wanted their child excused from singing could have their child remain mute during the songs, or work on a packet in the library to avoid exposure.

After that note went out, a well-dressed man in a pressed, dark suit strolled into the class after school, *"Mr. Ribonowitz. I'm a Jewish attorney who specializes in First Amendment law."*

> " *When knowledge from the two separate worlds intersects, that knowledge becomes far more important and interesting to the student. They'll retain that knowledge since it has important connections.*

Inwardly I gulped. Would I get sued over asking his son to sing songs that might mention Jesus?

"I want my son to sing those songs. He loves you and your class. I want him to learn about how slaves communicated. And I also want to tell you that you worded that note perfectly."

It made me happy to have an expert legal opinion delivered for free. And whenever I started a unit that could conceivably cause concern for any family, I offered a chance to opt out rather than get censored.

Helping Parents Reinforce Lessons

Your students live in two worlds. What they learn at school is quite different from what they learn at home. It's unlikely that they'll ever hear their parents discuss using commas around an appositive in a sentence, nor would they expect their teacher to expound on the merits of a certain game console.

When knowledge from the two separate worlds intersects, that knowledge becomes far more important and interesting to the student. They'll retain that knowledge since it has important connections.

If you can involve parents in what you are teaching at school, you become a more effective educator. This is why you want to send home specific information and questions for parents to ask their children.

> *If I used every parent volunteer in a constructive way, these parents will be my biggest cheering section.*

You can have students role-play parent and child to practice this before taking the questions home. For example, you could tell parents to expect their child to answer these questions:

> ▸ What are two different ways of adding or combining several two-digit numbers?

> ▸ How did slaves pass secret messages using songs?

> ▸ What are three kinds of sentences that we found in our class novel?

During our Back-to-School information night, I tell parents to look for questions that I email home each Friday in the newsletter. These questions can be the beginning of a family discussion where the child holds some expertise.

When kids see that what they learn in school is connected to their home life, learning becomes easier and forgetting becomes harder.

Volunteers

During the pandemic, few schools were allowing parents to enter the building to help out. If your building allows in-school volunteers, read this section.

I was teaching fourth grade in the high poverty part of the district. I put out a call for a room parent to help me organize and manage the class parties, but no one answered. Most of these parents were working long hours at minimum wages and unavailable to volunteer.

I would need to do the parties myself. I was talking to a parent of a first grader, and she said she'd be happy to help out. All I would need to do is to take care of the treats, plan and set up games and/or holiday crafts, and lead the activities. She said she'd do the rest.

It was nice to have an extra pair of hands for those parties, but I was doing basically everything.

Then I transferred to one of the highest income schools in the district. Sharon, a teacher experienced in teaching in such schools, gave me the information I needed to take advantage of the volunteer resources at my new school.

She explained to me that often parents in high income areas want to be involved with their children's education. If I used every parent volunteer in a constructive way, these parents will be my biggest cheering section. Parents will see me as a highly capable, professional educator, and they

> *It's important to make parents understand that their contribution is important, so they will continue to volunteer and support your students and your teaching.*

will be much more likely to listen to my advice. In essence, using volunteers will increase my effectiveness.

Here's what Sharon had me do:

> On Back-to-School night, have a volunteer sign-up sheet. List all the jobs that I think a parent might want to do. These should include tasks that involve working with children, tasks that do not involve working with children, and tasks that can be done at home.

> It's critical to get a parent to agree to be a volunteer coordinator. This person does all the calling, scheduling and organizing. If a parent has signed up to read with students on Monday at 11:15, that person calls the volunteer coordinator when she needs to get a sub. Getting a coordinator will save you hours each week on the phone.

If a parent comes in to help, and there's nothing for them to do, this makes you look bad and the parent wonders why she bothered to get a babysitter when there wasn't anything for them to do.

> Maintain a volunteer tub of tasks that need to be done. It's vital that this tub always has tasks for your volunteers.

Tasks might include preparing materials for an upcoming unit, duplicating papers you'll need, cutting out letters for a bulletin board, and so forth. You should have a variety of tasks ranging from clerical to working with kids.

Sometimes you'll want to put some fancy candy in your volunteer tub with a big thank you note. If a parent comes in to help, and there's nothing for them to do, this makes you look bad and the parent wonders why she bothered to get a babysitter when there wasn't anything for them to do. It's essential that you have this volunteer tub full.

I avoid giving parents a job like running a small group or anything that involves instructional planning. I do let them monitor stations. It can get messy if you need to "fire" that volunteer if you're not happy with how the task is being done.

› For parents who want to work with kids, what I did was to have parents come in during the sustained silent reading period and pull kids out for vocabulary development. For example, Mrs. Sato would come in each Monday and pull the same 4 students one at a time. I would suggest not having parents pull a group of students, unless you are certain they have the skills to manage the group.

Mrs. Sato and the student would go to the library and read a book of the child's choosing. Let's say the book was set on a ship. Mrs. Sato and the student would spend time discussing some non-fiction books on ships to help the students gain the background knowledge to fully comprehend the story.

These parents were trained to make brief notes in a journal about their time with the student. I would sometimes write notes back to the parents with encouragement or suggestions. You want these parents to be independent and not disrupt the class each time they come in. Provide a secure closet or drawer where volunteers can leave their belongings.

› It's important to make parents understand that their contribution is important, so they will continue to volunteer and support your students and your teaching. These will be the parents who will keep in touch with you long after their child leaves your class, and sing your praises to the other parents while chatting on the soccer field.

Some schools will not have parents who are able or willing to volunteer, but if volunteers are available, it's good management to use them effectively.

What did you learn in school today? Nothing.

Children often give this answer to a general question from parents. I think they do it because it's hard to pull up a cogent answer that will satisfy parents. Some parents might wonder if their child is learning anything at school.

> " Be sure to send out a newsletter that has been carefully proofread. If you have errors in grammar or spelling, it will weaken your image.

I suggest you end the day with this same question: What did you learn today? Depending on how much time you have, you can do the *Team Brainstorming* activity to generate some really great answers. Also, you get your student's perception of what they learned. This can give you valuable feedback for tomorrow's lessons.

Think of other ways to ask this question. If you are short on time, use *Two Stars and a Wish*. Students had to think of two things that went well at school, and something they wished had (or hadn't) happened. They share these thoughts with a partner or the class.

This part of the day is especially important if you have gifted students in your class. In order to calm concerns of fervent parents, I make certain that gifted students have a strong answer to the what-did-you-learn question.

Classroom Newsletter - Three Elements to Include

If you communicate with your parents, they will be more likely to support you and your educational goals for their children. They will be less likely to embrace misinformation if they feel they understand your goals and teaching. Your newsletter can be the bridge between you and your families. Some teachers accomplish this with weekly/daily texts, other than with a weekly printed or emailed newsletter.

I always take a tone as an expert educator, and each issue contains advice on how a parent can help with whatever we are working on in class or information on the developmental stages their child is going through. You want your parents to view you as a top educator who has their child's best interests at heart. If you can accomplish this, parents will be more likely to take your advice, thus helping you with your goals for your students. Parents can help you refine your goals as well. Communication can and should go both ways.

Be sure to send out a newsletter that has been carefully proofread. If you have errors in grammar or spelling, it will weaken your image. Follow district privacy guidelines on including student names and images. I also send home a photo release form so I only include photos of students whose parents approve. Look for advice from experts to include in your communications. Keep these short.

11
Lesson Design

TOPICS ADDRESSED IN THIS CHAPTER

LESSON DESIGN PRINCIPLES

THEMATIC TEACHING AND BUILDING CONNECTIONS

IT'S ABOUT THE CONNECTIONS

Designing an effective lesson is good classroom management. You want to have all your supplies prepared, your procedures mapped out in your mind and crystal clear goals for the lesson.

Lesson design is also a topic that could justify a whole book, but here are some general lesson design elements. Apply these and others to your teaching.

Of course, good lesson design emerges when you have an instructional goal for your students. This goal could come from your observations and other assessments, a state curriculum guide, school traditions, or other sources.

Study the topic of lesson design in depth in order to plan strong, effective lessons. You do not always use each of these steps, but adapt these principles to your content, time and students'

You do not always use each of these steps, but adapt these principles to your content, time and students' needs.

needs. Some of the suggestions in this list come from the studies of Dr. Madeline Hunter.

1.   Before teaching

Make sure you have all the materials your students will need. Have a slide or poster with the state learning targets written out and the lesson activities where students can see what to expect. You want to do this because students are much more likely to master the lesson content if you tell them what you want them to learn. Motivation goes up when students learn that their state expects them to understand the content and success criteria are clear. This is also the time to decide where to put movement into your lesson.

2.   Anticipatory Set

Start by connecting your current lesson to a previous class or students' personal experiences. This suddenly makes the lesson relevant to your students, and studies show kids learn best when new knowledge is connected to what's been previously learned. Once you activate prior knowledge, you can tell students what you want them to learn. If practical, have your students make predictions before or during the lesson. This will trigger curiosity and foster wonder and confidence.

I like to have their predictions written, but allow them to edit their predictions as they learn more. These predictions transition to knowledge. During this part of the lesson, you may discover that your students need additional background knowledge to be successful so you can make adjustments to your plans.

3. New Information

You can begin instruction by posing a problem and seeing what your students already know or can figure out. Deliver your instruction

> *Let's say your lesson is The Themes Present in Charlotte's Web. If you can get a student to name the themes, other students will view the information as easily attainable and motivation goes up.*

in an active way. Don't just reel off facts, but engage students by asking them to do mental and physical actions during the lesson. For example, have them compare the new information with the old, have them rank new knowledge by various criteria, tell them to think, imagine, ponder, differentiate and other mental processes as you present the new information. Use lots of questions. Let's say your lesson is The Themes Present in *Charlotte's Web*. If you can get a student to name the themes, other students will view the information as easily attainable and motivation goes up.

4. Presentation

As you present, you can use highly effective formative assessment by posing lots of questions and combining this information with your observations. Good teachers monitor their lessons and make adjustments. One sure way to make sure your students disengage or even misbehave is to have a lesson that is too hard or too easy.

Physically move your students at least every 20 minutes, or keep the lessons that short.

Your presentation is where you model the thinking you want your students to adopt. For example, you think out loud so students can see how you approach a problem. You might say something like this, "*When I look at this problem I think to myself, this reminds me of yesterday's problem except that it has this new part. I know I need to solve that new part separately then apply the result to what we learned yesterday . . .*" What's amazing is you are actually teaching your students HOW to think by thinking out loud.

5.   Monitored Practice

After you deliver the new knowledge, the next step is monitored practice. Have your students practice skills, manipulate the new information or solve problems as a class, in small groups, in pairs or individually. Often this concludes with a class discussion of their observations. This is a place for student exploration and discovery. Encourage students to explain their thinking to classmates since this is the essence of learning.

When students are practicing, you have a chance to differentiate instruction for students who need it or provide additional support for your struggling learners.

6.   Independent Practice

Next is the independent work aligned to the learning target, where students complete an assignment individually as you roam about the class. This can also be homework. Make it a practice to begin homework in class so no student goes home unprepared. This assignment might be explaining what they've learned, practicing skills, planning an investigation and so forth.

7.   Closure

This final, and important component is where you help your students make connections that will help them retain the new knowledge. Closure also

If you frequently check for understanding with your students, you don't need to offer many formal quizzes to feel confident in what you know about your students.

creates a feeling of completion and satisfaction in your students. It makes your class a pleasant place to be and encourages students to feel good about what they've learned.

8. Assessment

You want to understand what everyone has learned to plan the next lesson, arrange for remediation or acceleration. This means you must find out what your students need. Assessment can be done informally by your observations during the class discussion, as you roam and answer questions, with the results of the student work when you correct it, with a quiz or using other assessment techniques. If you frequently check for understanding with your students, you don't need to offer many formal quizzes to feel confident in what you know about your students.

Five Ways to Close A Lesson

Closure

This final, and important component is where you help your students make connections that will help them retain the new knowledge.

1. Students brainstorm what they've learned or add to the collection they made prior to the lesson when they compiled what they already knew about the topic. Collect and combine elements on these lists to use at the start of the next lesson.

2. Students summarize, apply or demonstrate their new learnings—written or orally to a partner.

3. Students examine, edit, and share their pre-lesson predictions. You can have them do this on a post-it, and place the post-it (with their name on it) on a door as their ticket out. These post-its are also an assessment device.

4. Students explain what they've learned to a partner, and then you call on a student to explain what his/her partner said.

5. Students list, in order of importance, what they've learned.

Thematic Teaching and Building Connections

Look up at the ceiling right now and name the five Great Lakes. I'll wait while you do that.

Most people will be able to quickly name a few of them, but struggle with others. If you are aware of the mnemonic HOMES, you probably got them all right away. HOMES stands for Huron, Ontario, Michigan, Erie, and Superior. At the end of this section, I'm going to ask you to look up at the ceiling and name the lakes. I'll bet you'll do it perfectly. Why not practice that for a moment before you go on with this section?

When you construct your lessons so various domains are intertwined—thematic teaching, it makes it easier for students to recall and use information because numerous connections are built into their brains that makes knowledge more accessible. Also, you want to connect your lessons to your students' existing cultural knowledge. When you do this, students not only learn and retain knowledge better, they see you as an understanding adult.

It's About the Connections

Sometimes you can help students make connections by digging deep into a unit, then use the learnings from that study to compare to all future studies. The techniques and language of the initial study can form a structure that helps students make connections intuitively.

> *As you teach, be sure to ask students to compare and contrast any new knowledge with what's been previously learned.*

An example of this is when my fourth graders studied the "verbs of attribution" (VOA) used by the author CS Lewis.

My fourth graders called these "said words". So when they attempted to write dialog like CS Lewis, they used mostly *said* and *asked* just like CS Lewis writings. For example, *"Pass the tea," said Lucy.*

When we started studying Beverly Cleary, their *Said Word* collections grew to include, whispered, screamed, mentioned, called, and so forth. Lewis didn't believe in using a vivid VOA, because he felt that the dialog should clearly convey the attributional tone to the reader, so that a descriptive VOA would be redundant.

After the Beverly Cleary unit, students began noticing the author's VOA in our next novel unit without any urging on my part. Just two units had solidified the connections and they were noticing literary elements without any prompting on my part.

As you teach, be sure to ask students to compare and contrast any new knowledge with what's been previously learned. A meta-study by Robert Marzano found that the most effective teaching strategy is to have students compare and contrast. This is due to the brain connections built.

I would add to Marzano's list anything that compels students to interact with their new knowledge. For example, have students decide which is most important and least important. Have them rank or group new skills or vocabulary by some criterion, or organize new information using a Venn diagram.

An example of this might be when given new math vocabulary words and the set of previously learned vocabulary words, students put the words into groups, and then label the groups to show their connections. A student might say, "I put subtraction and division in the same group because division involves subtracting same size sets."

Brain connections definitely work. For example, if I asked you to look up at the ceiling right now and name the five Great Lakes, I'm sure you can do it.

Topics Addressed in This Chapter

12

About this Book

" *Throughout my long career where I was selected for district, state and national teaching honors, I loved coming to school each day and seeing my students.*

All my life I ached to be a teacher. Right out of college I was hired to teach first grade in a high poverty metropolitan area mostly populated by children from very low income homes. I prepared to enter my dream job. After a month of attempting to teach, my principal, Mr. Lester, called me into his office and explained I would be fired at the end of the term due to my lack of classroom management skills. I felt crushed.

Crushed and relieved. I knew I was failing my darling, poverty-stressed students, and being fired would take me out of the chaos of my first class. I lacked management skills.

It turns out I did learn how to manage my class before Mr. Lester fired me. Throughout my long career where I was selected for district, state and national teaching honors, I loved

coming to school each day and seeing my students. Now I teach young educators at the college level, and love that, too.

Perhaps you want to learn how to be an effective classroom manager. This book is for you. In it, I included many of the key strategies I've learned on my journey from desperate ineptitude to joyful competence.

> *I regard the teaching profession as one of the most important jobs on earth.*

Why This Book?

If anything, the pandemic of the 2020s has taught us something important about education: that one of the most important persons in a child's life is their teacher. A teacher possesses the power to completely turn around a lost child, ignite a passion for learning, and set a child on the right path for a successful life.

The teacher can be a role model that leads to significant emotional development in a child. A teacher can be the one, powerful influence that guides a child to a successful life. A low-skilled teacher can also have the opposite effect.

However, when students in high poverty areas, living in highly stressed homes, lag behind the achievement of middle and upper income children, popular media often wrongly blames the teachers for these learning gaps. Teachers have nearly no sway over the home lives of these impacted children, and should not blame themselves for forces beyond their control. What teachers can do is be their best selves. It's with that in mind that I wrote this book.

I regard the teaching profession as one of the most important jobs on earth.

This book is all about supporting teachers as they develop effective classroom management strategies that will allow them to take their students as far as possible.

The path to strong emotional health is often through success as a learner. When a child finds and recognizes academic success, they get a burst of confidence that allows them to adopt and embrace the positive emotional traits modeled by their teacher: empathy, persistence, kindness, curiosity, and confidence. For this reason, academic success is strongly linked to emotional health.

I'm nearly certain that many of these strategies in this book would eventually be learned as someone spends sufficient time in the classroom and seeks out information, but I hope this book can fast-track that professional wisdom.

I want to give new teachers a quicker path to successful teaching and to help experienced teachers find some solutions that have heretofore escaped them.

What is Classroom Management?

The word, *management* can have negative connotations. In this book, classroom management means teacher actions that affect student learning. Some educators differentiate management practices from instructional practices. I focused this book on management, yet I believe management and instruction are inseparable. Instruction is crippled by weak management and boosted by skillful management. Powerful and effective instruction is largely dependent on management.

What This Book is Not

This book is not a comprehensive study of the subject because classroom management is just too deep for one source. As you go through these pages, you may notice I suggest areas of further study on a number of topics. This book is intended as a start. It's not the last one you should read.

There are many ways to solve the complex management problems that present themselves to a teacher, and this book gives you my views on how to solve many of them. However, you can faithfully follow my directions and find these don't work as well for you as they have for me. Just because these techniques worked for me, does not mean they will also work for your personality and your class make up. Thus, I would urge you to adapt the suggestions in this book to your style and talents.

> " *You may notice that certain suggestions come up several times. This use of repetition is intentional because I don't expect all readers to read each chapter, but to pick and choose what to read.*

Who Should Read this Book

This book is about what I've learned about classroom management over my career. I've taught every grade level from 1st to 8th and spent 30 years training teachers. Most of my classroom time has been in the upper elementary world, so I draw most of my examples from that area. For the last 12 years, I've supervised student teachers and practicum students in scores of classrooms from K to 12. View the lessons in this book as a start. Teachers of K - 1 will find lots of value here, but there's so much about early childhood education that I left out due to space. No matter what your grade level, I expect you to adapt my suggestions to your situation.

Unfortunately, our culture often quotes George Bernard Shaw's line, "He who can, does; he who can't teaches." as a way of disparaging teachers. It's unbelievably far from the truth. Just like there are smart people who could never be a great politician, comedian, or salesman, they can learn the skills and apply effort—but just not be effective.

There are well-intentioned people who could never be a good, or even adequate teacher. It takes a set of natural attributes and acquired skills to really teach well. This book focuses on the set of skills an emerging teacher can develop to really thrive in the job. Veteran teachers who want to gather fresh skills should also read this book.

This is a book intended for practitioners, not researchers. As a result, I have not included footnotes nor cited many specific studies. If you are skeptical about any suggestions or claims in this book, I suggest you give free reign to your curiosity and do some research. Browse the references and books suggested at the end of this book.

How to Use This Book

Examine the *Table of Contents* to see if there's something that really jumps out to you as useful in your teaching situation. If you read that chapter and find value, explore the other chapters.

You may notice that certain suggestions come up several times. This use of repetition is intentional because I don't expect all readers to read each chapter, but to pick and choose what to read. I also want to show how my suggestions work in different ways and under various scenarios. Also, some teachers, like me, learn with repetition.

In this and some previous chapters, you may notice I include some case studies and model teachers. In a perfect world, I could take you, my reader, to classrooms to observe and learn from amazing teachers. But this is just a book. I learned most of what I know about classroom management from talking with and observing other teachers and adapting their techniques to my teaching. See if you can use these chapter elements to plant the seeds of how improve your teaching.

Covid/Pandemic-Stressed Students

A huge public health crisis robs children and adults of the comfort of routine. Some children, especially from low income families, are highly affected by a pandemic-caused chaos. These particular kids will benefit the most from a safe classroom (See Chapter 2). At-risk students, whether the cause is a pandemic, poverty or something else, need capable, caring adults to provide a feeling of safety and comforting routines. Studies have shown that access to trusted adults can help children build resilience and overcome the effects of "adverse childhood experiences." Kids need their teachers.

What if You Try Something Suggested in this Book and It Doesn't Work?

Keep in mind, no matter how skilled a classroom manager you are, it's possible to have a student or students who are so emotionally or behaviorally disabled, that they appear unmanageable. These students can force you to drastically alter your teaching just to get through the school year. They can make you feel like a failure.

> *Skillful teaching takes years of practice to fine tune.*

If you find yourself in such circumstances, you need to seek help from administrators, colleagues and counselors. You need to be kind to yourself in order to get through the year intact. Forgive yourself for making mistakes and learn from them.

My turning point came that morning Mr. Lester taught a brief lesson in my class. My students behaved perfectly, and I saw how he did it. Using the techniques my principal demonstrated and building on them, I retained my job and grew into a competent teacher. In this book, I explained what I learned from him and techniques I discovered and developed afterwards.

Some teachers start out with such a powerful intuition about management, that they don't really think about what they are doing to make their teaching effective. I'm not a natural. I must think about what to do. As a result, I've learned I have an understanding of "what's going on under the hood" and find myself able to explain management to my student teachers.

Teaching as Art

Teaching is an art. Not everyone can do it. Skillful teaching takes years of practice to fine tune, and new teachers should not expect to become an expert instantly—even if they read this book. I remember reading a study that showed teaching skills improved steadily for the first 20 years in the classroom, as a teacher developed mastery. I've taught some brilliant, dedicated novice teachers who just needed some time to hone necessary skills.

Give yourself free reign to explore the assertions I've made and take your teaching far beyond what I've learned.

Newly minted teachers need to be patient as they learn the craft, but also recognize that it might be possible that they are not cut out to be a teacher. Some people should not attempt to become a salesman, a politician or an actuary.

Teaching is not for anyone. It requires some built-in talents and lots of motivation to become effective. There's no shame in leaving the profession if you decide you just don't have what it takes.

Your class composition, native skills and abilities differ from my experiences, so feel free to adapt any suggestions to fit your teaching style and situation. I'm hoping you'll see something in this book that causes you to develop a related management technique far beyond anything I could imagine.

It's also OK if you disagree with any of the assertions in this book.

Don't let any disagreements prevent you from learning something new from this book. My assertions and suggestions are based on the sum of my knowledge, research and experiences, and I do not claim to have the only way to solve classroom problems. These are what works for me.

> **"**
>
> *I'm hoping you'll see something in this book that causes you to develop a related management technique far beyond anything I could imagine.*

12
Conclusion

Throughout these pages, I have shared the most effective classroom management techniques that I've been able to learn. These have come from many teachers and researchers before me as well as my own lucky stumbles as I progressed from an inept novice to a highly-skilled professional. Give yourself free rein to explore the assertions I've made and take your teaching far beyond what I've learned.

I want to conclude with a description of a model teacher in her second year of teaching. This might be a model you would like to learn from, just as I learned to start a journey of strong management based on watching Mr. Lester teach a lesson in my class. As you observe Ms Rodri-guez's actions, think about the strategies and hard-learned lessons I've presented so far. Decide which of Ms Rodriguez's actions you would like to apply to your teaching.

Teacher Model: Ms Rodriguez

Sitting in the back of the room, I observed Ms Rodriguez, one of my former college students run a class discussion. I was impressed with her technique. It seemed the whole class was fired up and engaged. This was in huge contrast to what I'd seen her do much earlier in her student teaching.

I was especially impressed with her *Engagement Language* and use of *Wait Time*.

Engagement Language and Wait Time

When Ms Rodriguez first started, she would often say something like this after presenting information; *"Would anyone like to comment on this?"* Or *"Anyone think they know what might happen next?"*

The soft nature of her language allowed students to avoid engaging in the lesson. After all, she said, *"Does anyone . . ."* To class daydreamers that meant someone else would answer. Surely that smart girl in the first row will say something.

Ms Rodriguez's language also expressed a lack of confidence that her students would be able to respond. *"Does anyone . . ."* means she wonders if it's possible for her students to answer. All her timid students will keep their mouths shut since their teacher doesn't think they would know the answer.

Today she was saying things like, *"OK, we saw what happened with A and B. I want you to raise your hand when you have an idea of what might happen with C."* Then she would wait. She waited with her hand in the air to show students she expected students to raise their hand when they had prepared an answer. Her expectant smile showed she had confidence in their ability to answer her question.

She also used the words, *"I want you to . . ."* Since most students are born to care about what their teacher wants. Teachers are accessing deep parts of students' brains when they say things like, *I want you to . . ., I need you to . . ., It makes me feel happy when you . . ., I'm disappointed you choose to do that,* and so forth.

Ms Rodriguez showed me she understood this when I would often hear her explain to students what she wanted them to do and feel.

> " *The nature of her language allowed students to avoid engaging in the lesson. After all, she said, "Does anyone . . ." To class daydreamers that meant someone else would answer.*

Going back to Ms Rodriguez's question about what happened with A, B and C: after Ms Rodriguez asked the class the question, she noticed that only half the class had their hands up. To Ms Rodriguez, this meant they either lacked the information to answer, or the confidence to raise their hands. Before calling on anyone, Ms Rodriguez knew she had to either

1) provide more information so everyone could prepare an answer, or

2) give some confidence to the students who were unsure.

Ms Rodriguez reached over and picked up a cup containing popsicle sticks with student names on them. This added pressure for her students to engage. Her students knew she was about to draw out a stick to have a student answer. They would want to be prepared.

> " *She had the a critical element of classroom management solidly fixed: aim for 100% engagement when presenting information.*

Ms Rodriguez then told her students to find out what their sharing partners were thinking. Students had assigned partners arranged in 3s, so students would need to move in order to confer with them. This added movement to her lesson.

After, giving them enough time to share, then repeating her call: *"Raise your hand when you think you know the answer."*

This was followed by enough wait time to make sure every hand was up. Students expected that Ms Rodriguez would wait until their hand was up, so students without a solid answer were genuinely curious about what their more confident classmates were thinking.

Ms Rodriguez, like most teachers, would need several years of teaching before she could use all her techniques intuitively, but she had a critical element of classroom management solidly fixed: aim for 100% engagement when presenting information, and this meant she should use language which nurtures student participation. I'm sure no student will be daydreaming when Ms Rodriguez's teaching.

Helping Stressed and Delayed Students Catch Up

This topic should be covered in another book, but the most effective catch-up strategies involve: 1. Creating and maintaining positive relationships and prioritizing student engagement. 2. Teaching grade level curriculum. 3. After hours and weekend acceleration classes. 4. Tutoring from skilled staff in very small groups.

Money to pay for these interventions can flow to districts by ending state support for charter and voucher schools which have proven over decades as ineffective and wasteful. (Cowen, 2022) It's not time for politics, it's time to help our kids.

Books for Support

Brillante, Pamela, and National Association for the Education of Young Children. The Essentials : Supporting Young Children with Disabilities in the Classroom. National Association for the Education of Young Children, 2017.

Dinnerstein Renée. Choice Time : How to Deepen Learning through Inquiry and Play, Prek-2. Heinemann, 2016.

Grisham-Brown, Jennifer, et al. Blended Practices for Teaching Young Children in Inclusive Settings. Second edition. Paul H. Brookes Publishing, 2017.

Haberman, Martin, et al. Star Teachers of Children in Poverty. Second ed., Routledge, 2018.

Jensen, Eric. Teaching with Poverty in Mind : What Being Poor Does to Kids' Brains and What Schools Can Do About It. Association for Supervision and Curriculum Development, 2009.

Marzano, Robert J, et al. Classroom Management That Works : Research-Based Strategies for Every Teacher. Association for Supervision and Curriculum Development, 2003.

References/Articles

Bicard, D., Ervin, A., Bicard, S., & Baylot-Casey, L. (2012). Differential Effects Of Seating Arrangements On Disruptive Behavior Of Fifth Grade Students During Independent Seatwork. Journal of Applied Behavior Analysis, 45(2), 407-411.

Brenna Hassinger-Das, et al. "Reading Stories to Learn Math." The Elementary School Journal, vol. 116, no. 2, 2015, pp. 242–264.

Edutopia.org

Cowen, J. (2022, September 1). "Apples to outcomes?" Revisiting the achievement v. attainment differences in school voucher studies. Brookings. https://www.brookings.edu/blog/brown-centerchalkboard/ 2022/09/01/apples-to-outcomes-revisiting-the achievement-v-attainment-differences-inschool-voucher-studies/

Fay, Jim, and David Funk. Teaching with Love & Logic : Taking Control of the Classroom. 1st ed., Love and Logic Press, 1995.

Gilliam, Kyle, et al. "Effects of Question Difficulty and Post-Question Wait-Time on Cognitive Engagement: A Psychophysiological Analysis." Journal of Agricultural

Education, vol. 59, no. 4, 2018, pp. 286–300.

Hansen, Bruce. "Is the Bluebird Really a Phoenix? Ability Grouping Seems to Rise from the Ashes Ad Infinitum." Reading Today (Newark, Del. : 1985) 25.6 (2008)

Hansen, Bruce. "Teachers at Low-Income Schools Deserve Respect" Education Week (Bethesda, MD: February 9, 2016)

Hansen, Bruce. "The Day Reading Became Play.(a Teacher's Goal to Lead His Class to View Reading as Play)." Educational Leadership, vol. 67, no. 6, 2010, p. 78.

Jussim, Lee, and Kent Harber. "Teacher Expectations and Self-Fulfilling

McGillicuddy, Deirdre, and Dympna Devine. "'You Feel Ashamed That You Are Not in the Higher Group'—Children's Psychosocial Response to Ability Grouping in Primary School." British Educational Research Journal 46.3 (2020): 553-73. Web.

Prophecies: Knowns and Unknowns, Resolved and Unresolved Controversies." Personality and Social Psychology Review, vol. 9, no. 2, 2005, pp. 131–155.

Ogle, Donna, and ProQuest. Academic Vocabulary in Middle and High School : Effective Practices across the Disciplines. 2016.

Rosenthal, Robert, and Lenore Jacobson. "Pygmalion in the Classroom." The Urban Review : Issues and Ideas in Public Education, vol. 3, no. 1, 1968, pp. 16–20

Sorhagen, Nicole S. "Early Teacher Expectations Disproportionately Affect Poor Children's High School Performance." Journal of Educational Psychology, vol. 105, no. 2, 2013, pp. 465–477.

Stahnke, R., & Blömeke, S. (2021). Novice and expert teachers' situation-specific skills regarding classroom management: What do they perceive, interpret and suggest? Teaching and Teacher Education, 98, Teaching and teacher education, 2021-02, Vol.98.

www.stopbullying.gov

Lucariello, Joan M, et al. "Science Supports Education: The Behavioral Research Base for Psychology's Top 20 Principles for Enhancing Teaching and Learning." Mind, Brain and Education, vol. 10, no. 1, 2016, pp. 55–67.

Vrij, Aldert, and Bush, Nicola. "Differences in Suggestibility between 5-6 and 10-11 Year Olds: The Relationship with Self Confidence." Psychology, Crime & Law, vol. 6, no. 2, 2000, pp. 127–138.

Index

Symbols

A

B

C

D

E

F

G

H

I

L

M

Acknowledgments

It seems I always learn more from my students than any other place, but their intention was not to teach me. People who did teach me were all the amazing educators with whom I've worked. This includes colleagues that include Professor Dan Woods, Jeff Wright, Josh Ernst, Kelly Hansen, and most of all Sharon Hansen. Among other things, she taught me how to manage volunteers at my high-income school placements, and as a master teacher herself, her support helped me power through this book.

Thanks also to the many colleagues, researchers, professors, teachers of the year, and others who read and offered helpful feedback and support for this book.

Made in United States
North Haven, CT
13 January 2023

31035666R00122